To Annette,

Have fun Reading,
eating and enjoy
your life!

JUST THE COOK

The Trials, Tribulations and Recipes from a Catering Chef

By
Chef Clyde Serda

Copyright © 2006 by Clyde Serda

ISBN 0-7414-2939-X

Published by:

INFINITY
PUBLISHING.COM

1094 New DeHaven Street, Suite 100
West Conshohocken, PA 19428-2713
Info@buybooksontheweb.com
www.buybooksontheweb.com
Toll-free (877) BUY BOOK
Local Phone (610) 941-9999
Fax (610) 941-9959

Printed in the United States of America

Printed on Recycled Paper

Published January 2006

-FOREWORD-

This book sits on the same shelf as my most cherished pieces of literature from my legal notes at Harvard University, political science lecture material from Oxford University, Military Science business tactics of West Point Military Academy, entrepreneur advice for my business "A Sip and A Taste" from my mentor Donald Trump, classical Italian fencing diagrams of Accadema Nazionale Di Scherma, mental competitive training technical notes of the United States Olympic Shooting Team, car racing instructions from my coach Mario Andretti, culinary recipes from Le Cordon Bleu and my Chef Instructor Julia Child, and Order of investiture procedures from the Royal Crown for the honor of Knighthood.

This book is a masterpiece that alas proves that the pen is mightier than the sword.

Congratulations to you, the reader, who has found this rare find of literature, and three cheers to the Author— Chef Clyde Serda—for this wonderful work.

Bravo!

Sir Roy Joseph Salazar , Knight of the Royal Majesty
Certified Executive Chef, Certified Culinary Educator, Certified Master Taster

Chef Clyde Serda is passionate about food and delights in serving the palates of others. In *Just the Cook*, he turns his talents to writing a caterer's behind-the-scenes account of dinner parties: real food for sometimes surreal people. From the plates of a master chef to the tables of the rich and festive—and all the slips in between—Chef Clyde recounts back stories from elegant weddings and sit-down birthday parties to BBQs and $20,000-a-plate political events—and then provides us with the menus and his delicious recipes, so we can enjoy these feasts ourselves.

Marie Perucca-Ramirez
author and restaurateur

My old pal, Chef Clyde Serda, is a natural-born teacher. I've known him since 1994, when he was a friendly voice at the Help Desk for the American Culinary Federation National Convention, which our local association was hosting in San Francisco. At the time, he was advising people on where to go and steering them in the right direction. Since then he has been doing the same thing in his years at the California Culinary Academy and in his private cooking classes and food demos.

I once had the opportunity to get some very important guidance from him. I was scheduled to do a food demo, and my inbred stage fright was killing me. Clyde said, "Look, They Don't Know. *You* know the material; just go ahead and present it." His advice gave me confidence, and I was able to go on without a problem. So read on, Clyde has a lot to share!

Chef Ian Morrison
Executive Chef, Certified Master Taster
President
Chefs Association of the Pacific Coast
San Francisco

-ACKNOWLEDGMENTS-

I would like to express my gratitude and love for the people who have guided me in my culinary career. My mother, Marina Serda, who bestowed her cooking skills to me at my early age—teaching me to taste, taste, taste. My wife, Sophia, who has always given me both her love and support, has always told me to follow my heart, and was always eager to try something new or revisit the old.

To Mary Forslund, who without her help and coaching, I would have never begun writing articles, and has tried to teach me the proper use of "its and it's." To Chef Ian Morrison, who has been one of my best friends and culinary companions, whose booming "Yahhh" in the kitchen means that all is well, and who is always striving to make it better.

The following chefs have freely given me part of their soul and passion for food: Chef Otto Sommerhalder, who taught me the classics and always had faith in me; Chef Mial Parker, whose words still resonate through my head, "Hot food hot, cold food cold, must taste delicious." To all of my former students, at the California Culinary Academy and elsewhere, who taught me as well.

I would like to express a special thank-you to all of the members of the Chefs Association of the Pacific Coast, who have always expressed their gratitude and interest in my writing over the years. And to all of my clients, who helped make this possible.

October 2005
Chef Clyde Serda
Alameda, California

-ABOUT THE AUTHOR-

Chef Clyde Serda is a graduate of the California Culinary Academy in San Francisco. A former Chef Instructor at the California Culinary Academy, his field of instruction was food anthropology. He authored and instructed *Food of the Americas.*

He is a member of the American Culinary Federation (ACF), and Past President and Chairman of the Board of the Chefs Association of the Pacific Coast (CAPC) in San Francisco. He writes a monthly Education Article for *The Culinarian*, the official publication of the Chefs Association. He has written many reviews for culinary textbooks and cookbooks for various publishing houses.

He was honored as the CAPC "Chef of the Year" in 1996; received the National ACF Presidential Medallion awarded for his education articles; was recipient of the prestigious "Antonin Carême Medal"; and served as a member of the Carême Medal, Board of Trustees. Chef Clyde has earned several gold, silver and bronze medals in various types of food competitions around the country.

Chef Clyde has performed on several live cooking television shows and is a featured chef instructor on the PBS series and cookbook *In the World Kitchen, Global Cuisine from California Culinary Academy,* and helped author their *Wrap & Roll* cookbook. Chef Clyde has also contributed recipes and notes to several other cookbooks. He has taught more than 3,500 culinary students professionally and hundreds of individuals privately. He is a former Restaurant Chairman for the American Heart Association of San Francisco. Chef Clyde has personally raised thousands of dollars for various charities in the San Francisco Bay Area.

He now has his own business, "Chef Clyde," as a food consultant and a chef instructor both privately and at culinary schools. Chef Clyde is a Certified Master Taster and a culinary event coordinator. He is currently working on his second book, *History in the Eating*.

-PREFACE-

Having catered and prepared meals in hundreds of homes and at various events during my career, sharing many of the different, funny, sad and shocking stories with my friends and colleagues, I have finally taken their advice and put it all on paper.

As a Chef Instructor at the California Culinary Academy in San Francisco, I was called upon to teach various Continuing Education (CE) courses on the weekends. A CE course is a hands-on cooking class, where professional chefs share their talents and culinary techniques in the kitchens of the Academy on the weekends with the public. That's where I came up with the idea to provide cooking classes in private homes, where the courses could be tailored to client's needs.

This opened up a whole new business as a boutique, off-site, personal caterer. At my events, it allowed me to be the focus of the event—not just the domestic or hired help as most caterers are viewed.

Most homes are just wonderful to cook in, and a few are exceptional—exceptionally small, that is. A major portion of the private cooking classes often involves dinner parties of 12 or less, such as birthdays, anniversaries, holiday parties, new kitchen parties, as well as, small and intimate company parties and one-on-one cooking lessons. It also gives me, as a chef, firsthand knowledge that "Foodies can talk the talk, but they can't walk the walk." Sure, they are all experts because they watch the "Food Channel." However, once in the kitchen, most—even those who say they know their way around a kitchen—couldn't keep up with the slowest of line or prep cooks in any restaurant.

Since I have worked as a cook, chef and chef instructor and also worked for several caterers, private clubs, restaurants, schools, hotels and as a private chef, over the years, all of this has provided me with more than a few stories and experiences to share.

Most of the time, the dinner parties or cooking classes go quite smoothly and are almost routine. I arrive, set up the kitchen, cook or demonstrate, get the food served, and clean up. Then, I say my good-byes and go on my merry way. However, after some parties, I laughed, fumed, or just shook my head all the way home.

Just ask any caterer or chef if they have any funny stories and be ready to laugh for an hour or so. But, don't laugh too hard; they may be talking about you!

For those of you who are considering hiring a chef to prepare a meal or having an event catered in your home, the more information you can share with the chef about your kitchen (be truthful), the event, food allergies or concerns, and, of course, the menu and timing, the better off both of you will be. The last sentence is paramount in making your dinner, party, or event a success; remember—you hired us to make you look good! Because, we would rather not have a story to tell about what went wrong. (Oh yeah, clear off your counters and give us some shelf space in your refrigerator.)

As a side note: For those who are going to follow my footsteps by becoming a chef or are thinking of attending or are presently in a culinary school, remember some simple advice: Every time you are tired; have burned or cut yourself; worked a holiday, a beautiful weekend, or your sixth fourteen-hour shift—just say either to yourself or out loud—**"The Food Comes First."** This mantra will not ease any physical pain, but it will help you to refocus and get through another shift. And welcome to our elite fraternity.

-Table of Contents-

Chapters

Chapter Menu Recipes

17 Passover Dinner

18 Cooking Demonstrations

19 Fire! What Fire?

JUST THE COOK

**The Trials, Tribulations and Recipes
from a Catering Chef**

THE HOUSE

-chapter 1-

I was working as the chef for a caterer at this particular time, and we were going to put on a formal sit-down birthday dinner for fifty. The location was a home located in the foothills just below Mount Diablo. We traveled up the road and turned off the main road, traveling for about a mile. It seemed weird that there were no other homes around. We thought we were lost, but the directions said, "Go farther than you think." After about 5 minutes of driving, we came to a huge stone wall on both sides of the road that went beyond our view, with a tall, wrought-iron steel gate. A speaker and video camera were on both sides of the gate. I rang the buzzer and said, "We are the catering company." The gate opened, and we drove over a small hill; there were horses what looked like racehorses in pastures and a large house with tennis courts and a small swimming pool. We pulled around and parked at the rear of the house. As I went to the door, a young woman came out and said, "You're at the wrong house; this is the servants' quarters." Everyone in the van just looked at each other and shook their heads. We were then instructed to drive over the next hill. As we topped the hill, we could see what looked like a mansion, like one you'd see on the cover of *Architectural Digest*. The stone-faced house looked like it had an eight- or ten-car garage to one side of the house, with a huge cobblestone driveway leading to the house. There were young oak trees lining the driveway and a large fountain in the middle of a well-manicured drive circle. We drove around to the back of the house, where the stables, tennis courts and pool were located, not to mention a good size putting green. I got out from the van and knocked on the door. I thought to myself,

"You don't see beveled glass on a back door very often, and if so, not on doors like these."

We entered the kitchen through the walk-in pantry, which was larger than most kitchens. Now, let me tell you about this kitchen. Most restaurant chefs would sell their firstborn for a kitchen like this. It was huge for restaurant standards and not even imaginable for a home. It had two large reach-in refrigerators and a small walk-in (a refrigerator that you could walk into). There was a full-size freezer, two 8-burner stoves with four convection ovens, two large double sinks, and a commercial dishwasher. They even had a deep frier, a small steamer, a 24-inch gas grill, and a 24-inch griddle. Over one of the stoves was a salamander (broiler) and a plate-warming shelf over one of the three stainless steel counters, which were on a slate floor. The kitchen was about 30 feet wide by 60 feet long. There was every type of blender, mixer, pot or pan you could ever want or need. *I was in heaven.* The owner came in (she was Swiss), and shyly said that she only used one burner (for Top Ramen). "Isn't that terrible?" she said, and laughingly I agreed. She didn't even know what some of the equipment was—like the bread proofing cabinet, bread warmer or salamander.

She showed the staff to the dining room, where our mouths dropped even farther than before. There was a table made of black walnut, which sat fifty, yes fifty, and all of the chairs had armrests! It had to be seventy feet long. The staff groaned, remembering that they had to serve it. Around the room hung artwork, all depicting some type of food painting, from an early etching of a pineapple plant to a huge wall covering tapestry of meat roasting after the hunt. It was like working in the Hearst Castle. I was informed that the guests were made up of some of her husband's employees and friends with a few of their relatives thrown in to complete the table. The menu that night was a simple one. She had her husband's birthday cake delivered, and the ice cream was also "her husband's favorite flavor." Hey, who am I to argue! One little quirk was that the water glasses had to be filled with only Evian water, each with a round slice of lime and ice. The dinner plates were plain white with a thin 24-karat gold rim.

The evening went very smoothly. We were ordered to make enough food for 58 persons. The other 8 were the full-time live-in staff, who came and ate at the heavy walnut kitchen table that could easily seat twelve. The staff consisted of their driver-mechanic, the butler, two house servants, two gardeners, and a husband/wife team of wranglers, even though the owners only stayed there about a week a month. They also had homes in Aspen and Maui. Their menu was as follows:

The House
-chapter 1-

Wild Mushroom Consommé

Tossed Green Salad with Aged Sherry Vinaigrette

Asian Pear and Glazed Pecans

Roasted Breast of Duck
with Bing Cherry Sauce

Wild Rice Pilaf

Sautéed Pattypan Squash

Birthday Cake and Butter-Brickle Ice Cream

THE MOTHER FROM HELL!

-chapter 2-

As a chef, if you're working at hotels, private clubs or as caterers, you will sooner or later do weddings. Not our favorite type of event, but it pays the bills. Usually there are no problems; the bride deals with the catering manager and all you have to do is order the food, cook it, present it beautifully, and perhaps serve it on a buffet. Every now and then, you may have a problem. Believe me, in my career, I have had more than a few. It's usually that the wedding party has more guests than the bride ordered food for, or they are running very late, mostly because of the inconsiderate, overpaid, prima donna photographers, who insist on taking thirty more photos than they need. Or there are vegetarians among the guests, and we weren't notified. Most of the time, it's not a problem, if you are doing the reception "in house" (at your restaurant, club or hotel). But, when you are catering "off-site" like at a private home, rented hall or park, it can be a big problem. Such as the "Mother from Hell."

It was a very hot August day; the mercury was going to top out about 104, and the night was not going to be much cooler at the Walnut Creek home where the wedding was going to take place. The house was surrounded by a huge yard, much of it rolling lawn with a very small deck. The tables were to be set up on the lawn and the buffet line on the deck. We arrived early to set up, since the entire ceremony was to take place at the home in the late afternoon. The minute we arrived, the mother of the bride came out in a jogging suit and curlers. I said, "Hello, I am Chef Clyde," and she replied, "Don't let your staff in my house. I have guests with valuables, and we don't want anything missing!" "Okay," I replied, as the staff said, "Oh, my God, is this going to be fun or what?" We began setting up the tables and chairs; the lawn was soggy from being over watered, and the excess water collected and pooled in the low spots in the lawn. The weight of the tables and the softness of the ground made the tables sink about 2 inches into the turf. The area that we were to place the tables had a flag in the turf where each table was to be centered on. So, we put them there— even though about 6 feet over it seemed drier and even a little flatter. As we were setting up, her husband (not the father of the bride) came out and asked for some food; he said, according to his wife, "You are supplying food for the day." I said, "No sir, just for the event." About two minutes later, stomping her way past the tables and the empty buffet line to the bar area where I was helping to set up, she screamed, "Look asshole, I paid for your services and that's what I want! You are paid to do the cooking!" I replied, "What do you want me to feed him? The steak, or chicken, but if I do, I won't have enough for the reception. You insisted we make just the count of servings you ordered, not any extra, because we wouldn't get paid for it." Just then, the wedding cake arrived. It was very nice, but I immediately saw a problem. It was covered in white chocolate and had all types of curls and chocolate ribbons decorating it. She told the decorator that she wanted it placed out on a table in view of everyone. I said, "The cake really should go inside where it's air-conditioned." She glared at me and shouted, "What the hell do you know—you're just the fucking cook!" I stepped back, as did the cake decorator, a bit shocked, who said, "Whatever you want, but I think the chocolate might melt in the heat." The mother said, "Just put it on the table," and she walked away. I told the decorator, "Neither I, nor my staff, will move it once the cake is set in place; we will only cut and serve it." She agreed.

Before the ceremony, the mother came up to me and informed me that there were 3 vegetarians who would be attending the wedding. I replied, "I don't have anything special for them, as we weren't notified." She said, "Okay, you can go into the kitchen and make something for them." I thought, "Yeah right, lady, I have 45 minutes before the ceremony and still have to get the appetizers ready." So, I went into her 'forbidden' house and into the kitchen, opened the refrigerator, and there was nothing in it—just wine and beer. So, I opened a few cabinets, and again, they were almost empty. She had an old spice rack and a couple of cans of soup—and not much else. There was a door that turned out to be a walk-in pantry, and on a shelf, there were some white onions, olive oil, dry cereal, a canister of rice and flour, along with 3 bottles of cocktail onions and mixed drink ingredients. Among them was a can of coconut milk.

I grabbed the white onions, olive oil and rice and went into the kitchen. I opened a drawer, which contained the spice rack, and luckily there was some curry (never opened). I boiled the rice, sliced the onion in half across the stem, and then, very thin crosswise, sautéed the onions until they were golden. I sprinkled some curry powder along with a little cumin, salt and black pepper on them. I then deglazed the pan with some vermouth, poured in the coconut milk, brought it to a boil, and just kept it warm. I served the curried onions over the white rice. It was beautiful.

The wedding was about to commence when the mother walked out of the house, wearing all black. My head server said, "Isn't that fitting?!" We both chuckled. The bride was a little heavy, and her very tight, cream colored, satin dress made her look like a bratwurst. As the ceremony was taking place, the father of the bride came up to the bar and wanted a drink, not just the champagne, but also a three-finger scotch. The bartender told me it was his third. He said, "This house was my dream, but the witch had a better lawyer," and then he walked away. Towards the end of the ceremony, we noticed that the cake had a tilt to it, and two of the five ribbons on it were folded over from the heat. The main server, with a look of fright on her face, said, "What can we do?" I replied, "Not much." I went over to the cake and propped up the ribbons, but the cake was beginning to slide. I didn't want to touch it for fear of having it fall apart. I tried calling the decorator on my cell phone, but there was

6

no answer at her shop. Just about then, the mother came to me and said, "You have to move the cake into the shade." I replied, "I am sorry, ma'am, but the caterers do not move wedding cakes—especially one that is ready to fall apart— but I will try to get it straightened up so you can move it." She raised her hand to pull her hair back, and that's when everyone noticed she still had the store tag under her armpit, wrapped in plastic, so it wouldn't smudge from her sweat. The head server quickly jumped into action and asked, "Should I remove the tag from under your arm, so your guests won't see it?" The mother said, "No, just deal with the cake," and walked away as if nothing ever happened. We got her husband and two other guests to move the table into the air-conditioned house where we were able to make the necessary repairs to it.

As the buffet line was moving, I noticed a very good-looking woman in her mid-twenties in line. She had shoulder-length auburn hair and a red dress with a white collar and trim. A few minutes later, I saw the same woman wearing a red and white, small-checked dress, again we said, "Hello," as she passed before me. About five minutes later, she appeared again, or at least I thought it was she. She was wearing a white skirt with a red belt and blouse, and I thought, "Nawh, I must be mistaken; she has got to be trying on different outfits." Towards the end of dinnertime, I noticed all "three of them" facing a sliding glass door which acted as a mirror each pointing to each other's outfits and giggling. I stopped dead in my tracks, triplets! I went over to them and said, "I thought I was going crazy when you were in line." They giggled and said, "We used to drive our teachers nuts since the three of us are identical." I asked them if they previously discussed what each was going to wear since the shades of red were the same color. They replied, "No, it just seems to always happen that way."

As the party went on, the drinking got heavy, and the heat didn't help. The guests were literally dancing on the tables and knocking them over. We were hired to keep the bar open until eleven, and it was just past that time. The staff was dragging, not only from the heat of the day, but also the stress of the party. We were all beat. We began packing up the bar and putting up the chairs and tables when the mother appeared, raised her arm, with tag still attached, and pointed to the bar and said, "Don't you tell me when we close the bar." She grabbed what was left from a case of wine and handed it out to her guests, and then grabbed and handed out a couple of bottles of vodka. The guests were slurring drunk and couldn't walk a straight line if they had to. We packed up the van and noticed that several of them were continuing to drink; they even banged on the side of our van as we were leaving, asking what else they could have. Another group of guests were pooling their cash and staggering over to a car to make a run to the liquor store. I grabbed my cell phone and called the County Sheriff's Office and told them that I was the caterer and that there were a lot of very drunk people who would be leaving the party from this residence. As we drove away and down the hill to the main road, we came across the sheriff's checkpoint, and we saw several of the guests lined up trying to walk the line. I sort of felt bad in spoiling their evening, but not for the memories of the "mother from hell."

The next day, the mother called the catering office and said she was contesting the bill because several mink coats were missing. I told her that she probably returned them with her dress.

The Mother from Hell!
-chapter 2-

Butter Lettuce Salad
with Champagne Vinaigrette

Curried Onions with White Rice

Roasted Breast of Chicken with
Orange-Pineapple-Gin Glaze

Roasted Beef Tri-Tip with Mushroom Vodka Sauce

Asparagus Spears with Toasted Almonds

Herbed Rice Pilaf
with Pine Nuts and Golden Raisins

THE FAMILY

-chapter 3-

I worked for a family in Orinda. They had two kids and a wonderful home on a hillside overlooking a huge duck pond. I cooked a dinner for them, usually one Saturday a month. They would invite a couple of friends over and have a nice dinner, enjoying their home and company. Often their kids would stay over at a friend's house or would stay in their rooms until dinnertime. Sometimes, one or both would sit in the kitchen with me while they ate, often watching me prepare the food.

Dinner was usually simple; it could be pasta, steak or chicken, but they liked having someone else cook it for them while they entertained. The husband was always on or off the Atkins Diet (way before it was popular). He was very wealthy. With a college buddy, they figured out banking software for ATM machines. So, they received a royalty of ¼ cent per transaction for a few years, and it didn't take long for the pennies to add up. They had 6 Mercedes-Benz vehicles in the garage and one minivan. One day while I was taking the elevator up to the house from the garage, I asked him, "Why not 7 Mercedes?" He smiled and said, "Even God took a day off." One of their favorite dinners was my Roasted Fresh Herb and Lemon Chicken, which I usually served with sautéed vegetables and tossed baby green salad with various types of vinaigrettes. The kids' favorite vegetable was Green Bean Bundles Wrapped with Carrots. Usually, I would prepare some type of pilaf or potatoes; their favorite was Toasted Orzo with Wild Rice.

The Family
-chapter 3-

**Salad of Baby Field Greens
tossed with Aged Sherry Vinaigrette**

Roasted Fresh Herb and Lemon Chicken

Green Bean Bundles wrapped with Carrot Ribbons

Toasted Orzo with Wild Rice

**Fresh Berries on Malted Waffles
with Soft Vanilla Ice Cream**

ONE-HANDED

-chapter 4-

One cold wet day in December, I was to prepare a special holiday luncheon that Brenda, a longtime client of mine, was putting on for a group of her girlfriends. I was in a hurry because I was running late. It had drizzled earlier that day, making the stairs at my house slippery. While carrying my last load of equipment, I slipped, fell and landed, hitting my elbow on the stairs—man, did it hurt! I knew it was broken, but my truck was loaded with food, and I had about one hour to get ready. I arrived at her house and recruited her son to help me unload and take the food up to the kitchen. I popped a few aspirins that I kept in my tool kit and began my preparations for their lunch, the whole time saying to myself over and over, "The food comes first, the food comes first." The luncheon menu consisted of:

**Butter Lettuce Salad, served with
Gala Apple, Pomegranate, Shaved Parmesan Cheese,
Croutons and Pomegranate Vinaigrette**

**Achiote Crusted Pork Tenderloin
served on a Bed of Spanish Rice and
Sautéed Chayote Squash**

To-Die-For Chocolate Mousse (shown)

Well, I got the salad and entrée out okay, but when it was time for me to pipe the chocolate mousse into the wine glasses, my elbow was so swollen and throbbing, I just couldn't do it. I called Brenda into the kitchen and asked, "Could I just spoon it in?" She asked me, "What is the matter?" I informed her that I thought I broke my arm just before coming over. She called in one of the ladies who was a nurse. Of course, all of them came running in. The nurse rolled up the sleeve of my chef's coat, took one look at it, and said, "You mean to tell me that you fixed us lunch with only one arm because this one is broken?" I said, "Yup, but now it hurts like hell!" They helped me spoon the mousse into the glasses, and Brenda's son loaded my truck, and off to the hospital I went to get my cast. By the way, that was the first and only time I ever left the kitchen or dishes unclean at a party.

I worked for them for several more months, each time enjoying their company and having them enjoy my food.

THE DRESS

-chapter 5-

All chefs have a few dishes they like doing over and over because they could prepare them in their sleep. It's fairly easy; even though to their guests, it seems like a difficult dish. For me, it's Rack of Lamb. Not just because it is very easy to do, but also because most people don't cook it at home, and if they do, it's overcooked. I love to cook for my friends, and often I am asked to help them with a charity or personal function. If I am available, I'm pleased to lend a hand.

This time it was a fund-raising dinner for a politician in another state. My friend asked me to prepare the dinner for them. It was a sit-down for twenty people, and they were donating twenty grand per plate. I was happy to do so. I made up the menu for her; she told me, "Nothing fancy, just simple and flavorful." So, my menu was:

Caesar Salad

**Herb Crusted Rack of Lamb
with Rosemary Demi-Glace**

Duchess Potatoes, Roasted Carrots and Sautéed Squash

Local Marion Berries with Rémy Crème and Shortcake

The dinner went fine; even though it seems that whenever I cook, the party always wants to come out to the kitchen to see what's happening, not that it bothers me. I love to put on a show.

Towards the end of the entrée, one western-dressed gentleman came into the kitchen, holding his empty plate, and asked if there was any more lamb. Luckily I had a few end pieces to offer along with an extra serving of potatoes.

After the dinner, a well-dressed woman came into the kitchen. She gave me a big smile, and said, "Chef, I wish to thank you for such a wonderful meal and my new dress." "Your dress?" I replied. She broke out into a huge grin and said, "Last week I was in San Francisco and saw the most beautiful dress. It was fifteen hundred dollars, and my husband said, 'No, way!' He was the guy that came in for a second helping of lamb. I told him that if I couldn't get the dress that I was going down to the coffee shop tomorrow morning and tell all of his friends (who know that he's the head of the Cattleman's Association) that he asked for seconds on lamb." With that, she gave me a hug and kiss on the cheek and walked out of the room.

I'VE HAD ENOUGH!

-chapter 6-

Have you ever worked for a person that you just wanted to get away from? I was working as a cook at a fairly large, local catering company. The owner, who was Jamaican, seemed nice enough when I interviewed with her. I was only looking for some part-time, fill-in work. I worked for her just a few days, making up her Jamaican appetizers, which I really didn't like the flavor or texture of, so I won't burden you with her recipe. When she came to me and said, "I hear dat you don't care for my food, mon." I replied, "It's not that I don't like it; I'm just not used to so much curry." She shrugged her shoulders, passed through the double doors of the kitchen, and walked out to the parking lot, got into her car, and drove away. The rest of her crew had their heads down working, like they were expecting something more to come of it.

Earlier, the owner, along with the chef, went over my daily prep list with me. I was to make up the remaining appetizers, make a gallon of red wine vinaigrette, a pasta sauce for 50, and get 10 loaves of garlic bread ready for the oven, all for a party that evening. After that, if I had time, I was to make another batch of pasties, her pirogi-style, curried appetizer filling. I had finished all of my tasks and was working on the filling, when the kitchen double doors were kicked open, slamming against the walls. She strode in, stood there with her hands on her hips, glaring at us. "I know dat yous sons a bitches been goofing off. I caught yous, didn't I?" The mostly Guatemalan and Cuban kitchen crew were used to her coming back with a half a heat on and just kept working, never looking up. I thought to myself, "What the hell?" She yelled, "You new-mon, you still working on dem pasties yet? Damn you slow." I replied, "They've been done, wrapped and stored, as well as the stuff for tonight." Both the sous-chef and chef agreed with me. The owner somewhat staggered past the kitchen into her office where she fell asleep. I later found out, that sort of thing happened a lot on Friday afternoons.

The next day, very early, we were making up two hundred box lunches. For the first few hours, I put together the boxes, while others made up turkey, roast beef or tuna sandwiches. We took a coffee break. I had brought a banana and "gala" apple for my lunch. With her Jamaican accent, she said, "Mon, you stealing my apples for da lunches, mon?" I looked at her, laughed, and said, "These are from home, Mon! Go count your precious apples." I picked up my knives and walked out. As I passed her, I said, "I've had enough!"

THE NAKED TRUTH

-chapter 7-

I was called upon to do a Thai Dinner Class in Berkeley for ten persons. One of the items that was requested on the menu was Green Papaya Salad. It was mid-summer, and I had a heck of a time trying to find green papaya—most were ripe to overripe. Finally, after a visit to Chinatown in Oakland, I was able to find enough of them to make the salad.

The two female hosts greeted the guests as they came to the door and showed them into the kitchen. The eclectic group seemed friendly enough; they joked and had a few laughs, as I handed out to each of the couples their cooking assignments and recipes. They all knew each other, but it was evident that they hadn't seen each other for some time. One of the hosts, shall we say, was an Amazon! She was a big girl, at least 6'6" and very curvy, but not overweight; the other, while shorter, was about 5'6", slightly stocky and very well endowed. Both hosts disappeared from the kitchen for a while. The other guests were busy performing their tasks prepping different parts of the meal in the very small kitchen. I thought the hosts were getting the dining table ready, as I had not yet gone into that room. After about twenty minutes, the two, now kimono-clad hosts, came back into the kitchen. The tall one had a long strand of fairly large pearls around her neck that draped just under her shoulder-length auburn hair and was carrying a long peacock feather; the other had a hot pink, rabbit fur, riding crop. Everyone chuckled as they were tickled with the feather or from the snap, as they were slapped across the butt with the pink crop.

A few of the guests, like most dinner classes I have given, weren't really interested in cooking—just in drinking, eating, and having a good time—which is okay with me. They're usually the ones that can't do anything right anyway, and I end up having to do it for them, trying to get their dish ready in time for service.

The wine and Asian beer were flowing, and we served the Green Papaya Salad. The next dish was Shrimp and Cilantro Soup with Fresh Thai Chile Peppers, which they did a good job of making. As the group plated up the soup, making small talk and joking, a few kissed. However, it seemed to me, they did not kiss the partners they came with, but I wasn't sure. All went back into the dining room, carrying in their next course. The music changed from '50s rock to soft new wave. The dining room went from overhead light to candlelight. It seemed to me that they all were enjoying themselves; there was some talking and laughing going on. I was in the kitchen cleaning up from the first few courses, looking at the clock, trying to figure out my exit time, and at the stove checking on the dessert, when I heard a giggle. I could just barely see into the dim candlelit dining room through a crack at the edge of the swinging door. I could swear that I saw one or two of the guests, and they had no clothes on. "Can't be," I thought, continuing to clean the kitchen and getting the main course ready.

The Amazon came into the kitchen, carrying a few plates, followed by her roommate and most of the guests. They were *all naked!* Not a stitch of clothing on them, except for a peacock feather one or two carried. I mean, I saw on some what no man should see! Saying "Hello!" They all laughed and said, "You don't mind, do you chef?" I replied, "No, so long as you don't burn yourself, I would put on an apron if I were you," looking to the guy next to the stove with his Johnson almost up against the hot oven door. One of the female guests, with more than a handful of love handles hanging on her sides, said, "We thought we would let you finish the dinner, if you don't mind?" "Okay, it's all the same to me," I said laughingly. I didn't want to look around; I just looked at the pot and asked for someone to hand me the plates, thinking, "Lady, get some clothes on!

And you with the back that looks like a grizzly bear—get a wax!" The Amazon was the only one who should even be allowed to go naked. She really had a full shape that was very proportionate to her height, and was the only one there whose boobs were where God intended them to be. She whacked her pink fur riding crop on the back end of a guy with no buns, making a loud snap.

I was glad when they all marched into the dining room, laughing and joyously carrying out their plates, and I was thinking, "Man, I am glad the Amazon insisted on paying me when I first came in." I had their dessert ready for them in the kitchen and poked my head in to say good-bye, noticing that all of the couples had changed places. And I was out of there, and that's the naked truth. The menu is as follows:

The Naked Truth
-chapter 7-

Green Papaya Salad

Shrimp and Cilantro Soup
with Fresh Thai Chile Peppers

Chicken in Green Curry
with Coconut Jasmine Rice
and Gingered Baby Bok Choy

Coconut Ginger Ice Cream

HER LAST MEAL

-chapter 8-

I worked as the executive chef for a caterer, located in a small town in the Bay Area. Although we were a small company, we did a huge volume—up to three weddings a weekend and with only a crew of 5, feeding about 1200 per weekend. We received a call, during which the owner came to me and asked me to go over the menu with the prospective host. The client was very exact in the way she wanted the food prepared and the serving time. She was also exact on how she wanted the staff to dress as well as the time of our arrival to her home; three hours before the party to insure that we had plenty of setup time. The waiter and helper were to be in tuxedo with tails and white gloves during service.

We arrived at her home in Moraga—a small, upper class, rural, college town. The host greeted us; she was in her mid-forties, thinly built but fairly attractive even without her makeup, answering the door dressed in jeans. She asked if this was all of the crew. The co-owner/waiter replied, "Just as you requested." She sat down on a chair, took a deep breath, and said, "This is going to be a dinner for myself and four dearest friends. This will be the last time we will be together. The five of us have been best friends since attending Saint Mary's College together over twenty years ago." Her face saddened as she said, "I have terminal brain cancer and have less than three months to live." We were shocked and just stood there, silent, just looking at her. "So," she said, "I want to go out with a bang! My doctor told me I can't fly, so I am flying my girl friends here from New York, Paris, Houston and Los Angeles, all first-class. I've put each of them up in a suite at the Mark Hopkins Hotel in San Francisco. Their limo should be here about 6:30. Please, don't make a fuss about me; we just want a perfect evening together." She let us know that she had no heirs and that she was trying to spend her savings before she left, as she was donating her belongings and house to her church. As I was getting the kitchen set up and doing some of the last-minute prep, the host would pop her head in and out of the kitchen, asking me how I prepared the various dishes that were selected. She explained to me at which restaurants or hotels she had them and why she liked them so much. She said that she wasn't much for fluff food, just a meat-and-potatoes kind of girl. Her list of eateries was very impressive, and I kept saying to myself, "I hope I can match it." I was very satisfied with the food I put out that night. I knew I had given my best to her, but I still think about her and her dinner from time to time. God rest her soul.

When the party arrived, they were dressed in full formal gowns, as was the host; all of them looked stunning, as if just coming from a salon. The dining room was formally set. The burning candles cast a warm glow on the gold-rimmed dishes. The chairs were covered with a gold tapestry fabric that matched the runner on the table. Well-chilled Dom Perignon Champagne was served along with a tin's worth of beluga caviar, which I displayed in a crystal bowl on ice, accompanied by toast points, chopped quail eggs and finely diced red onions. It was requested that the waiter say nothing to the guests during dinner and to be as invisible as possible. At each place setting, on the charger, was a small red velvet jewelry box for the four guests. As they opened their gifts, I could hear from the kitchen, their squeals and deep inhales, as only women can do, as each opened and saw the diamond bracelets the host had for them. "To remind you of me, every time you wear it." Neither the waiter nor the waitress could take it, and both came into the kitchen with tears streaming down their chins. "Man, you're lucky you weren't in there," the waiter said, wiping the tears from his face, as they both stepped outside to compose themselves. Nat King Cole was playing in the background, and the talk was steady and very cheerful. The four guests had two, full, all-expenses-paid days in San Francisco to get over the shock of the reason for the dinner. In the kitchen, I was set up and ready to send out the courses as required.

The evening ended with us packing up and going out the backdoor, never saying a word to the guests, as they sat on the couch talking and drinking coffee with their desserts. The host had left an envelope with me as I was setting up the kitchen—in it was a two hundred dollar tip for each, with a thank-you card. The menu was simple, but all of the dishes were the host's favorites:

Her Last Meal
-chapter 8-

Caesar Salad
very lemony and with plenty of
Anchovies and Sourdough Croutons

Individual Beef Wellingtons
served with Truffled Demi-Glace

Turned Roasted Red Potatoes with Rosemary and Garlic

Broccoli Florets with Orange Hollandaise

Strawberry Shortcake
served with Fresh Strawberries in Kirsch
and a Vanilla-Mascarpone Cream

THE BLACK NIGHT

-chapter 9-

Sometimes, as chefs, we see things that just boggle the mind, or in some cases give you a case of the heebie-jeebies. I took part in one of the scariest weddings I had ever seen, while working one weekend at the Corinthian Yacht Club in Tiburon. This club, which without question, offers the most beautiful view of San Francisco that there is. It looks like the Emerald City, across the shimmering San Francisco Bay, with its skyscraper skyline behind the waterfront, with Angel Island and Alcatraz off to one side in the middle of the Bay, and both the Golden Gate and Bay Bridges on each side of the view.

It was a very calm, warm, Indian summer day. There were no clouds, fog or wind, just a breathtaking view. The Corinthian's massive ballroom, where the wedding reception was being held, was draped with heavy, dark red and black embroidered drapes—totally concealing the million-dollar view and any possible sunlight from entering the room. There were tall silver candelabrums with large dark-red candles surrounding the room, blood-red tablecloths and napkins. The centerpieces were blood-red roses with black ribbons and smaller red candles. The room was lit only by candlelight, giving the room the gloomy look of a mortuary during prohibition, or a San Francisco whorehouse during the Gold Rush. (All of the kitchen and wait staff thought it looked like a scene right out of a vampire movie; some even walked around with their arms covering their faces and saying, "I vant to bite jour neckkk," while others walked around with arms held out, walking like zombies.)

The bridesmaids were dressed in long, black, lace gowns. Crimson ribbons were tied in bows around their necks. All were the type of people you may see on the streets, with the white heavy makeup, dyed jet-black hair and black lipstick; all of them cast a ghoulish look. The males of the wedding party wore black velvet tux with tails; each had a matching crimson bow tie and cummerbund over a black ruffled shirt. The guests were also dressed in dark colors, as were the musicians. It was very obvious that there were no white or bright colors anywhere in the room. I asked one of the musicians, "Is this a vampire wedding or what?" He replied, "There are a lot of dark souls here tonight." The hair stood up on the back of my neck, the same as when I went into a haunted part of a plantation outside New Orleans. I didn't like it, nor did any of the other staff; everyone just had a funny feeling about the whole affair. I was one of the banquet chefs that evening and was very glad that it wasn't a buffet, or that I didn't have to work a sauté station, so I didn't have to be near them. Just to make sure, I carried some garlic in my pocket. At the end of the night, which by the way was a full moon, I didn't waste any time getting away from the club as fast as I could.

PAELLA

-chapter 10-

It was early one fall evening when I received a strange call. The would-be client asked me, frantically, if I was Chef Clyde, and if I knew how to make paella. I replied, "Yes, but what type of paella?" I got her to calm down just a bit and found out that she was planning a surprise birthday party for her retired husband, who had just left for the store, giving her the chance to sneak in the phone call to me. She gave me a date; it was the Saturday of her husband's birthday. Unfortunately, I already had an event that day, so we went for the following weekend. Later during the week, she contacted me again, and we went over exactly what she wanted. She explained that, while serving in the Armed Services, her husband was stationed in Spain and was invited to the family home of one of the Spanish soldiers he had met. He had always talked about the wonderful look and flavor of this simple dish, and how he wanted to learn how to make it. I asked her, "How many people are you planning it for?" She replied, "For 8 to 10 people with some leftovers." I replied, "No problem, paella has a way of growing geometrically with each ingredient added to it." I quickly explained the history and origin of the dish and its main ingredients, which consisted of rice, saffron, chicken, Spanish chorizo, mussels, shrimp and onions. Also, many other ingredients can be added—such as garlic, parsley, pork, scallops, clams, fish, calamari, lobster and lemon slices; the list is endless.

At the party, the birthday boy, who first had the dish back in 1954, was more than eager to learn how to make it, closely following both the recipe directions and little tips I gave along the way. During this time, they snacked on an antipasto platter and were happily drinking sangria. A mutual friend told them that I was very knowledgeable in spices so they wanted to know about saffron and its history. I also explained the different types of paella, and that a short grain or Arborio type of rice should be used, although I have even used a parboiled long-grain rice. The important thing is that it is sautéed, to bind the excess starch. Also, you should use high quality saffron, preferably from Spain, not the Azafran from Mexico. If in doubt, just look at the price. During one of our initial chats, the hostess then explained to me that she had an electric stove, and since it was expected to be raining, I figured the cooking would have to be done indoors. The electric stove was a problem since paella pans are usually very thin metal. Normally, paella is cooked outdoors on a propane burner or stovetop with gas burners. Most electric burners allow only the rice to cook around the area of the heating coils and not evenly. With a thin paella pan, the rice would almost be sure to burn, where the heating coils touch the pan.

Cooking the paella became a little more involved than it needed to be. We cooked the chicken in a very large sauté pan, drained most of the oil, and then added the rice and later the onions. While the rice was cooking, we sautéed the shrimp and the scallops in another pan, then added the mussels. Usually everything is cooked in the same pan, just layering the ingredients during the cooking time. From one of her neighbors, we borrowed the largest ovenproof serving platter she had. We mounded the cooked rice, arranged the chicken and cooked seafood, drizzled their nectars over the dish, added some chopped tomatoes, and sprinkled chopped parsley over the top. We popped it in the oven for a couple of minutes, just long enough to bring it all back to temperature and placed the bountiful platter on the table. Along with the paella, we served some nice crusty sourdough bread, a spinach salad with an aged sherry vinaigrette, and good hearty Spanish red wine.

Paella
-chapter 10-

Sangria

**Crostini with choice of
Spanish Olive Tapénade, Roasted Pimento,
Roasted Garlic and Caramelized Onions**

**Baby Spinach Salad
Aged Sherry Vinaigrette
Spanish Olives, Aged Machango Cheese**

Paella Valenciana

DOES THE STOVE WORK?

-chapter 11-

Working for a caterer that only does off-site events makes you quickly learn the art of organization. After just a few of them, one finds himself needing a checklist. You just can't pop into the corner store if you forget something. One of the most important things I always asked the catering planners or managers was to find out what type of stove the host had, including how many ovens and do they all work? I learned early in my career to plan for the unexpected, and only the probable will go wrong.

We were doing a Christmas dinner at a newer mid-size tract home located in Danville, California. The menu was not one that I would have chosen for the event, but as the chef, I had little say in the matter. I just cooked what the contracts called for. The party was for 20 people, and it was noticeable that they were going to be very cramped in the small dining room. With a few tables and pieces of plywood, we were able to extend the length of the table well into their family room. The table did look great, with all of the Christmas decorations on the tables and the green and red plaid napkins that were trimmed in gold on a crimson red tablecloth. The gold chargers glistened with the candlelight, which also reflected off the crystal glasses.

Unfortunately, the kitchen was extremely small, and it had only one electric stove and small oven. I shook my head when I first saw it; I believe the words out of my mouth were "Awe man!" I asked the event planner, "Didn't you tell me she had a large kitchen?!" She gave me a glaring stare, snottily replying, "I never saw it." Horror of horrors, I went to the stove to try the burners, and out of the four, only one worked. I did, however, have four portable propane stoves and an electric griddle that I had brought with me (always plan ahead). But, I still wasn't out of the weeds. The menu called for Veal Piccata as the entrée, which is a dish that has to be cooked very quickly over high heat and served immediately, otherwise it becomes gummy. This dish is tough enough to make for a banquet in a restaurant kitchen. But in a home, with just portable stoves, this was a living nightmare. The oven was just smaller than my half-sheet pans (no one should ever buy an oven that an 18½ inch, half-sheet pan won't fit in) I was anticipating to finish cooking the vegetables and potatoes in it. Luckily, I did pre-roast the potatoes and blanch the vegetables back at our catering kitchen.

Did I mention that there was next to no counter space? I mean, there was only three feet of counter space in the whole kitchen, and the microwave took up most of that. I placed the microwave on the floor and pulled a table from the patio into the kitchen.

The soup course was made back at my catering kitchen, and there was no problem keeping it warm; the salad course also went smoothly, having pre-made the vinaigrette and prepped the fruit and salad greens, so that putting them together was no big deal.

I set up the battering station for the veal on the counter, and used one of her very small ⅓-size cookie sheets to reheat the potatoes and vegetables. I must have looked like a mad man, because the wait staff kept laughing at me when they came into the kitchen—from dusting a pre-pounded slice of veal in seasoned flour, placing it in the frying pan, turning the veal in the next pan over, taking another finished scallopine from the sauté pan, placing it on the electric griddle that was on low, and repeating the process on the four portable burners, like a whirling dervish, working in a circle around the kitchen. On the one working electric burner, I had some butter melting along with lemon juice and a little of the brown bits from the sauté pans. To the sauce, I would add some capers, turn the heat up, and drizzle some of the sauce over each dish. I was able to make up 6 plates on the almost useless stovetop and two on the open oven door. The wait staff knew not to cross my path, which could break up the sequence of cooking and plating. The catering owner/planner came into the kitchen. She was also waiting tables that night and asked me, "What's taking so long?" I replied, "One more word, and you better duck." We were able to complete the dinner, but it was one of the hardest events I ever did. I think this menu would be great for a weekend dinner for your family.

Does the Stove Work?
-chapter 11-

**Pumpkin Soup
with Toasted Pumpkin Seeds**

**Tossed Green Salad
with Pomegranate, Apple, Toy Box Tomatoes
and Raspberry Vinaigrette**

Veal Piccata

Sautéed Green and Yellow Zucchini

Roasted Yukon Gold Potatoes with Fresh Herbs

Fruit Cake and Holiday Cookies (by host)

NOT MY DOG

-chapter 12-

I do a lot of charity events. It's my way of giving back to the community and putting some points back in the karma bank (which I draw from frequently). Often I, as well as other chefs from the Chefs Association of the Pacific Coast in San Francisco, am auctioned off to prepare a dinner usually for 8 to 12 persons in their home. The menu is usually set, but I am usually flexible with it.

This dinner for 12 was auctioned for fifteen hundred dollars that supported a local San Francisco shelter, The Raphael House, a place for homeless women and their children to get back on their feet. The Chefs Association chose The Raphael House because it receives no state or federal assistance. It had been close to a year since the auction had taken place, and after several attempts the recipient and I were able to set a date for the dinner. It was to be held in a home in San Francisco, in a fairly expensive, upper middle-class part of the city. It was nice to see a lawn in San Francisco that wasn't just in a park. All of the homes had well-groomed lawns and impeccably maintained front yards. When we arrived, the hostess informed me that she and her husband were divorcing and that she was having her friends over. At the same time, her new 4-month-old bouncing Golden Retriever puppy gleefully greeted us. The host had purchased the puppy to keep her 6-year-old daughter company. Her house was nice; the small kitchen was remodeled with a modern look to it. Although a little short on counter space and a very narrow (what chefs call "butt to butt") aisle way, it was workable. In the dining room was a table with 12 place settings around it and a sea of crystal. My wife (God love her!) volunteered to help me with the dinner as my server and kitchen helper. I walked into the kitchen where she was working and laughed. She said, "What?" I said, "Have you looked at the dining room?" "No," she replied. We both walked into the room, and when she saw the Waterford crystal stemware, she said, "How am I supposed to serve the wine? There's no room! I don't even know if I can get around the chairs, they're packed so tight." I told her not to try to serve the wine, just to serve the plates and that we will put the wine on the table and let them pass it themselves.

Just as the evening's guests began to arrive, the host came running into the kitchen and asked me to help her open the chimney flue, smoke was coming into the living room! I found the handle and pulled the flue open, she said, "My husband used to start the fires." As guests arrived, mostly unescorted women, I brought out some cheese and crackers while they began bashing their ex-husbands. When all of the guests arrived, they sat at the table, and I sent out the first course. The blue crab cakes were no problem. The empty dishes were brought back into the kitchen, with one untouched. Next, was the salad course. There was a request for one with no dressing; that was easy to do. I should mention that I was always tripping over the puppy; it just kept lying at my feet. The kitchen had a hardwood floor that continued into the family room. So, I was able, with the side of my foot, give the sprawled puppy a gentle push, and she slid across the floor, never moving, just watching the room spin by. After about fifteen minutes, the plates returned; the one without dressing still had the crumbled blue cheese and toasted walnuts on it. My wife informed me it was the same lady who didn't eat the crab cakes.

I was working on the entrée when the puppy disappeared, although we didn't notice, until the host came into the kitchen. She moved us out of the way; we both figured that someone had spilled their drink, but she said, "Didn't you let the dog out?" "No," my wife replied, "we didn't know it had to go." We've both raised two retrievers and know to take a puppy out just after it eats, but we didn't feed the puppy. The hostess said, "I fed her just before you arrived." She got some paper towels and some cleaner and looked at us like, "Please go clean up the mess." We both kept on working after she left the room. I said, "Not my dog." Then I said, "I'll forego a tip and let her clean the poop," and my wife smiled.

The entrée went out, and when the plates were returned to the kitchen, one hadn't been touched. The same woman who hadn't eaten the crab cakes, cheese or walnuts told my wife, "I only eat micro-biotic food." "So, why come to a dinner, if you're not going to eat?" I said to myself. We served the last course, cleaned the kitchen, and left before we had to do the crystal, still laughing about the poop.

Not My Dog
-chapter 12-

**Chef Clyde's Southern Blue Crab Cakes
with Warm Creole Rémoulade**

**Baby Field Greens
with Dijon Vinaigrette, Crumbled Maytag Blue Cheese,
Toasted Walnuts and Granny Smith Apples**

Lemon Herb Crusted Rack of Lamb

Garlic Duchess Potatoes

Oven Roasted Asparagus

Triple Chocolate Torte with Rémy Crème

THE CRUISE

-chapter 13-

This adventure took place during another charitable event. I drafted two other fellow chefs to help me on this event—Chef Ian Morrison, one of my closest friends who was responsible for my involvement with the event, and another chef who was a co-worker of ours. This was featured as an Appetizer Cruise. It was sold to forty persons and included a lot of different wines and beer with eleven different appetizers, served both hot and cold. Chef Ian and I prepped all of the items ahead of time, but they still needed to be put together and, in some cases, cooked aboard the boat. Luckily, it had a very decent size exhibition kitchen, which opened up to the salon dining area. The three of us were making up the "apps" and putting things together as the guests arrived onboard. We greeted them and introduced ourselves. The boat finally got underway, and the guests were not at all shy about pouring themselves wine. As the night progressed, there was a guest who got louder and louder; he began speaking down to my fellow chefs and me. Saying things such as, "Where's the beef? Hey Chef Pancho, how many ways can you cook a chicken? Don't mess with my drink, I know you have been drinking my drink!" After about an hour of this, I was getting a little steamed. But he went topside, and we were left with several embarrassed but very friendly guests who were praising our food and efforts.

After a while, I toured the boat and went down below to the main stateroom. I could hear giggling as I climbed down the spiral stairway. There was a small but roomy cabin, which had five women standing around and sitting on the bed. They pointed to the bathroom, which had an enclosed red whirlpool tub, with red tile and gold faucets. There was also a mirror covering the entire ceiling of the bedroom. The bed had a red satin covering and pillows on it. There were also two guys down there. I looked around, smiled, and said, "The captain said all husbands overboard," and the ladies all laughed, looking at the guys as they said, "You heard the captain."

The salon area was getting a little stuffy from the heat from the chafing dishes and sauté station, as well as the body heat from the guests, so I went topside. The drunk was there. He took a couple of steps toward me and started right up again, saying, "Hey Chef Poncho (this time, he got it in the ribs from his wife), what's for dessert?" I told him, "This is an appetizer cruise, and dessert is not on the menu." He replied, in a shouting voice, while pointing his finger at me, "Well, why the fuck not?" I worked my way over to him and spoke into his ear, "Another word from you, and I'll gut you like a catfish!" He looked shocked, walked away, and sat down at the far end of the boat; he never spoke another word to my fellow chefs or me that evening.

The Cruise
-chapter 13-

HOT HORS D'OEUVRES
**Tiburon Point Crab Cakes served
with Warm Creole Rémoulade
Apple Wood Smoked Bacon with Dates and Almonds
New Red Potatoes with Chorizo and Cumin Cream
Crostini with Sun-dried Tomato Tapénade topped
with Brie & Mango Chutney** (shown on cover)

COLD HORS D'OEUVRES
**Ahi Tuna with Wasabi Cream and Ginger Caviar
in a Cucumber Tower
Nawlin's Style Shrimp with Tangy Cocktail Sauce**

JUST A SONG AND A DANCE

-chapter 14-

As a private chef, we are often asked by our clients not to tell anyone that we work for them or to give their name. This is often written into the contract under the privacy clause. This also goes along with many other clients. Although no formal contract is given, a verbal agreement is often reached between client and chef. This was not the case with a dinner I did in the very exclusive Pacific Heights neighborhood of San Francisco. The house was built at the turn of the century, but was recently remodeled; from the kitchen, there was a view of a small but beautiful garden that could have been on the cover of any *Sunset, Home and Garden* or *Leisure* magazine. It was perfect in every detail, from the deep green lawn to the bounty of color splashed here and about, with a small slate waterfall and fountain in the background and a petite patio with wrought-iron furniture and well-padded seat cushions.

The dinner was for ten persons. The hostess chose a menu with an Asian flair to it. When I arrived, I was greeted by the young, very attractive hostess, who informed me that this was her mother's house, and her mother would not be attending the party. I proceeded to get the kitchen and my equipment ready, as well as the food set up and prepped for the dinner, even as the early guests arrived. Of course, like most dinners, the guests migrated into the kitchen just to see what's going on. It was also the place where the wine was kept. Three stunning ladies in their late twenties were enjoying their wine, when the doorbell rang and a screech was heard, "Cammy is here." A tall thin blonde with skin-tight, red, satin pants walked into the kitchen. All of the girls hugged and immediately broke into this song and dance.

They were singing a tune something like, "It's too big to fit in here, too big to fit in there." I had never heard it before. They were making dance moves, like cheerleaders, slapping their own and each other's bottoms (not one of them being more than a handful), and holding or touching other various body parts, as the song went on. I kept thinking, "I know this face, I know this face," but I just couldn't put it together. The mother who was still in the kitchen, shook her head, and brought out an old photo taken of these young girls. I was told that Cammy had just finished a picture in San Francisco, and that it was great to see her with a few of her close friends again. The mother grabbed her coat, then smiled, and told me that she was banished from her house, but she would be back later that evening.

It was about an hour since the first guest had arrived, and the entire group was having a good time both in the kitchen and living room. I served the first course, and as it went out, I was grateful that the host had hired her mother's house cleaner as a helper for me in the kitchen to keep up with the dishes. I was pleased to see that all of the dishes came back clean, because as a chef, I always try to see what comes back from the dining room; it's our first key that there is something wrong. Often, you'll see the starches coming back, especially since the Atkins rage took over, but as a private chef, I have been working with that diet for clients for many years.

The dinner had barely begun, when the mother came back home, actually she had only been gone about an hour. She said that she went out for Chinese food and a movie. I said, "Either I'm slow, or the movie was short." She replied, "No, the movie was bad, as was the food, so I left early." She looked longingly at the food I was preparing and told me it looked much better than what she had eaten earlier. I offered her a plate, which she willingly accepted, and pulling up a stool to the counter, she ate, saying, "Oh, this is so good." She asked me questions on how I prepared the various dishes and watched every move I made. We talked about various local restaurants and the types of food we both liked as the night went on. Actually, it was nice to have someone to talk to during my presentation of the dishes (it makes you very conscious of how the dishes should look). At the end of the night, I got a hug from Cammy, and she told me to call her; I went home smiling.

Just a Song and a Dance
-chapter 14-

Tiger Prawns and Scallops
on Baby Bok Choy

Spring and Bitter Greens
with Hoisin Vinaigrette

Teriyaki Chicken Skewers

Asparagus Tips
with Water Chestnuts and Black Bean Sauce

Chocolate Ice Cream
with warm Snickerdoodle Cookies

THE WEDDING CAKE

-chapter 15-

As I mentioned before, one must plan for everything to go wrong at an off-site event, and you'll go away happy if it doesn't. We were to cater a wedding that was being held at one of the local city-owned halls; it was a small reception with only fifty persons. We packed up our van with the cooking equipment, linens, plates and glasses, food and champagne, and along with the crew headed down the freeway, where we ran into some heavy traffic. An accident had just happened, and as we slowly drove by, we noticed the van on its side. The logo on the van's backdoor was that of one of the more well-known cake makers in our area. We arrived at the hall; the bride's mother asked us if we knew what time the wedding cake was to arrive. We all looked at each other. "What cake decorator did you hire?" I asked, and she replied, "Cakes Plus." I told her that we had better call the bakery. Sure enough, it was their van and her cake, literally, on the side of the highway.

The bakery owner had just received the call from her driver, and was panicky and in the process of looking up phone numbers to try to get a hold of the bride. The bride's mother looked like she was going to pass out. We sat her down, and I said, "Don't worry, we'll think of something."

I jumped into the van while the catering crew was setting up and went to the local Safeway supermarket and explained to the baker what happened. He scooped off the Happy Birthday frosting from two round cakes, one smaller than the other. He re-frosted them in white, and sold me a wedding cake stand for the second tier and the two cakes. I picked up a dozen red roses from the flower stand and a couple of bars of Hershey's chocolate at the checkout stand on my way out.

After about a half an hour, when I got back to the event, I took the chocolate, melted it, and put it into a piping bag that I had formed from some kitchen parchment paper. I was able to pipe strands of chocolate across the cake, as if it was Silly String. I tore off the petals from a few roses and sprinkled them over the cake. They stuck wonderfully to the warm but hardening chocolate, and I surrounded the top layer's bottom with rose buds. It was beautiful. The guests never knew what happened and we received a heartfelt thank-you from the bride and her mother, as well as a healthy tip for our efforts.

I have found that in a kitchen, chefs must always keep their heads during an emergency and show a sense of calmness, which also eases your staff. Otherwise, it takes panic to the next level. It helps to also always go by my golden rule, "They don't know," and most of the time, they think it's the way things should be. (Although, when it happens in the kitchen, it's a crack-up to hear the chef yell, "We're all going to die," or "We're doomed; we're all doomed.") Later that evening, we found out that the driver was okay. She had a blowout in the front tire by running over a piece of metal on the highway, hit the rail, and turned the van over. However, they needed to get a new van.

IT'S A BARN!

-chapter 16-

The catering company was hired to do a huge off-site event for a local charity. The event was to have three hundred attendees; the theme was country-western. We were able to do most of the food prep at the catering kitchen. We had been informed that there was no kitchen facility at the event, just two huge portable barbecue pits. We only needed the pits to finish cooking the chicken and to cook the tri-tip steaks.

When the catering crew arrived, all of us just stood at the huge open barn door where the event was to be held. Dee, the head of the wait staff, kept saying, "It's a barn, a damn barn," while we unloaded our van. There were hundreds of chairs set up in auction fashion and about 40 round tables and chairs each set up for eight persons. The wait staff was "ticked-off," which is a kind word for the mood they were in. It was well over a hundred degrees outside, and in the barn, it seemed even hotter. The floor was dirt, and the great hall or barn was actually an indoor riding arena, and you know what was in the dirt, all broken up and ground in. You couldn't walk without stirring up a cloud of dust with each step.

The tablecloths were red and white checkered, as well as the napkins. Mason jars were set at the table as glasses to drink from; I had the wait staff turn them over to try to keep them clean. It didn't take too long before the chairs, tables and linens had a fine covering of dust on them. All of the wait staff's shoes were black and covered with dust and other particles. The banquet line was going to be inside, but I felt that it would be too unsanitary for me to serve the food inside; however, the decorator and host insisted. We set up our tables with rows of chafing dishes and covered everything with linen, trying to keep it clean. There was a bar with more than a few kegs of beer in ice-filled washtubs and a country-western band setting up. They seemed to be used to the dust and smell. Even before the first guest went through the buffet line, my sparkling-white chef's coat was grey. There was also a dance floor at one end of the arena. I asked if we could set up the buffet line there. "No," was the answer.

We had a problem of getting the briquets started. They had washed down the barbecue pits, and they still had a lot of water in them. We got them going and fired up my portable propane stove to heat the corn on the cob in a 20-gallon stockpot, dressed the salad, and put out the corn bread, after filling the chafers with food. Over all, the party went over very well, and everyone liked it (except for us), plus we had plenty of compliments on our food.

It's a Barn!
-chapter 16

Tossed Caesar Salad

Garlic Buttered Corn on the Cob

Slap Yourself Corn Bread

Maple Baked Beans

Grilled Lemon Achiote Marinated Chicken Breast served with Margarita Sauce

Chef Clyde's Texas Dry Rubbed Tri-Tip served with Chipotle Barbecue Sauce

Self-Help Strawberry Short Cake

PASSOVER DINNER

-chapter 17-

First, I should mention that I am not Jewish. I have had the pleasure of participating in the ceremony of Passover dinners on two occasions, many years ago, one of which was Kosher and I was the catering chef. The other, I was a guest of a friend.

The Passover dinner that I first prepared was during my stint as the chef, for an off-site caterer. This dinner was to be prepared at our catering kitchen and served at a Danville home. Like all of the homes in the gated community, it was large and beautifully decorated, both inside and out. Our hostess met with us at our kitchen to go over her menu and food requirements. One of the requirements was that our kitchen be shut down for three days prior to the event for cleaning, which meant not taking any parties over the weekend. We had to include our loss of profit and labor for the three-day shutdown. She asked as part of the contract that we have our kitchen blessed; after agreeing to that, we were informed that all of the dishes (and there were lots of them), glassware, silverware, pots, pans and cutting boards were to be supplied from a Kosher rental house. We just had to tell her the amount and what we needed. The good part on renting dishes is that we just had to scrape them off, keep them separate, and place them back in the same containers they came in. We were instructed not to mix them up, or they would have to be destroyed or sold to another rental house. We also had to order our meat and poultry from a Kosher butcher.

The week of the dinner, a rabbi and his assistant came into the kitchen. He told us that we could stay or could come back in about an hour. We elected to stay and watch.

Putting on his scarf, he began about an hour's worth of singing and praying, which was fine; that's all we thought there was to it. Then, the assistant took out a huge blow torch, lit it up, and began heating up the three stainless-steel work counters; he held the torch until the section he was heating turned blue. As our eyes got bigger with each pass of the torch, more prayers were said. Then the rabbi asked for my knives, I looked at him, straight in the eye, and said, "No way, you'll ruin the temper of them; we'll buy new ones for the dinner." Before the owner could open her mouth, the rabbi said, "That will be fine, leave them in the plastic they come in, until you start cooking." He packed up their things and left. He also said that since we weren't a Kosher house, he would be sending his assistant to watch so that we used no other unblessed equipment to prepare the meal the next day when we were going to do the cooking. I don't remember what the menu was, but to me, it didn't seem like it was worth the expense of the whole procedure. However, I do remember that it did give the hostess of the party bragging rights in her kitchen, about the cost of it all, to her guests.

Recently, I again had the pleasure of cooking another Passover dinner. This one, however, did not require the strictness of having my kitchen blessed, but did require me to stay within the guidelines given to me by the hostess. This was only the second time I ever made matzo balls, and well, actually, all of the dishes in the menu. I decided that although the dinner was very simple to make, following the recipes that were provided by the hostess, they seemed bland just from reading them. I asked the hostess that if I followed her guidelines about the ingredients, which I could and could not use, did I have her permission to bump up the flavor? She agreed. I figured that if I used the matzo flour in place of flour to dredge and brown the meat in the tsimmes, or stew, it would add another dimension to the dish. My chicken soup was a hit. I was told by a guest, "It's the true test of a cook." "I don't know about that, but I do make a mean chicken soup," I replied. And of course, there is always the frail old lady, who slowly made her way into the kitchen. Holding on to the counter as she walked towards me, she patted me on my arm saying, "The soup was very good, but those matzo balls—I can tell you're not Jewish," with a wink and a smile.

I think every chef should know how to cook dishes from several different cultures. As a chef, it's our culinary experience that allows us to go beyond the recipe and into the realm of flavor, allowing us to make dishes still authentic, but have them just taste a bit better.

Passover Dinner
-chapter 17-

**Chicken Soup
with Knaidels and Carrot Pearls**

**Salad of Tender Field Greens
with Toasted Walnuts, Dried Cranberries,
Golden Beets and a Shallot Vinaigrette**

**Oven Roasted Asparagus
with Pumpkin Seed Oil**

**Tsimmes
with Chicken & Beef**

Chocolate Toffee Crisps

Strawberry Rhubarb Crumble

COOKING DEMONSTRATIONS

-chapter 18-

If you're a chef of any notoriety, you will eventually be asked to perform a cooking demonstration, be it at a culinary or cooking school, street fair, county fair or food show. Over the years, I have not only done hundreds of cooking demonstrations, but have also put on complete shows at major food shows. It's always a pain to line up twenty different chefs and try to fulfill their kitchen needs when all you are supplied with is a stove and maybe an oven. This is where planning comes into play by having a bevy of kitchen equipment ready for their use. No matter how well you plan these two- or three-day events, you're bound to have one or two chefs not able to attend at the last minute or some type of equipment failure. Most of the time, things run fairly smoothly with the audience in awe of the chef displaying his or her talents. Oh, I have had more than a few problems; usually it's the traffic or parking situation that make the chefs late for setup. Usually when this happens, they are flustered, and it shows onstage, as they try to rush to catch up with the clock as most of the demonstration times are posted. When a chef runs late, I try to just juggle their time with a chef who is early. If I have no one to fall back on, I always have at least two demonstrations of my own at the ready. Sometimes it's a simple fruit or melon carving, how to sharpen a knife using steel and a tri-stone, how to use the knife properly, or how to cut vegetables. It never fails that someone always asks, "How do you keep from crying when you cut onions?" Answer, "Simple, hire a chef." I always find it amazing at how, in the last 15 years, with the help of the Food Network, television has propelled the chef to superstar status. Not that we aren't, but more people pay closer attention to how food is prepared and what better than a free cooking lesson.

As a chef, it's always good to have several dishes in your back pocket that you can easily explain and still have some depth and flair to them. The dish should be simple enough to be made at home. It can even be a common dish, but with a talented touch, taking it from ho-hum to restaurant status.

If possible, know the history of the dish and give several variations to it, explaining how easy we can change the flavor ethnicity just by adding or omitting an ingredient. Try to have a finished dish with the tasting portions ready to just reheat if needed. Put a finished garnished serving on a fancy plate or charger. (I like big plates for demos.) Have most of the ingredients prepped, so all you have to do is a small amount of cutting or chopping. Try to always have something to cut or chop; this allows you to show off those knife skills.

Here are several dishes that I have demonstrated over the years; all of which were always crowd pleasers. Always make sure you have enough for them to taste and copies of the recipe. One thing I have noticed, observing other chefs, is they fail to clearly explain each step and act as if it was a race to get it done. Take your time, speak loudly and clearly, and look at them, not just at your cutting board. If you use a kitchen term, explain it. I have always found that if a chef is nervous, I will help him or her out by asking questions about the ingredients or procedure; knowing the answers, this helps to calm a chef and gets the information out to the audience or class. Having done more than my share of cooking demonstrations, yes, it's a pain to pack up everything. But, they have come to see *you*! And that's the next best thing to getting them in your door.

Cooking Demonstrations
-chapter 18-

Asian Shrimp Patties with Thai Green Curry
Blue Crab Salad with Creole Dressing on Baby Greens
Calamari and Penne Pasta with Saffron Cream Sauce
Crusted Pork Tenderloin & Dry Rubs
Dungeness Crab with Ginger and Garlic
Panko Crusted Salmon with Mango Papaya Salsa
Pan Seared Sea Scallops in Pepper Vodka Sauce
San Francisco Cioppino

FIRE! WHAT FIRE?

chapter 19

This event happened during my time as a Chef Instructor at the California Culinary Academy in San Francisco. It was Friday, and every Friday there was a grand buffet for lunch and dinner in the prestigious Carême Room. I had the morning class, which put out the lunch for a full dining room, ranging from 150 to 300 guests, depending on the day. All week the class puts out an à la carte lunch, while designing the menu and theme for the grand buffet.

This particular week, we were going to have prime rib as the primary meat, along with roasted ham and turkey, as it was an English Banquet. Also, on the menu were Yorkshire puddings, which are nothing more than batter, oven-fried in popover molds, using the fat from the prime ribs. It was about 10 minutes before the buffet was to open; one could see the pack of blues (blue-haired seniors) waiting in the lobby, looking through the glass doors and exhibition windows. The meats were all out on the cutting boards; the hot food buffet line with the various starches and vegetables went through the kitchen, allowing the attendees to view and speak with my students while being served.

All of a sudden, there was a lot of yelling, "Chef, Chef, fire! Chef, fire!" I looked over across the kitchen where a thick black smoke was billowing out of the farthest oven in the kitchen. The oven had been turned up to 450 degrees to make the Yorkshire puddings; however, someone had spilled a bunch of grease from the previous class, that was pooled in the bottom of the oven and had gone way past its smoke point and ignited. I grabbed the sparkling white tablecloth that was covering a prep table, which housed the onions and potatoes below it, shoved it in a sink that was filled with water, and squeezed out the excess as fast as I could, then grabbed and handed a fire extinguisher to a student who was standing a few feet from the oven, and calmly told her, "Hold this, do not pull the pin, hand it to me when I ask for it." She looked really frightened; her hands were shaking as she nodded her head. I asked the closest student to the oven what was in there. "Nothing," was the reply. I grabbed the folded kitchen towel from my back which I kept tucked in my apron (to keep dry) as a pot holder, shut the oven off, opened the door from the side, and stood back, as flames shot out from the burst of air, and then they pulled back into the oven. I quickly pulled the lowest oven rack out, which was closest to the grease flames, and closed the door with my foot. I took the wet tablecloth, folded it into a square, had a student open the door where the flames again shot out, and tossed it in the oven, covering the flames, and closed the door with my foot. The black smoke went white with steam, and I said, "Who's the new Pope?" The fire was out. The class just stood there looking at me. I looked around the kitchen and bellowed, "You have one minute before service—are all stations ready?" The buffet went smoothly, and no one, but the students and the laundry man, ever knew what happened.

After service, I had a class meeting, and we talked about the valuable lesson they had been part of that day. Some were still a little shaken, but all realized that you have to stay calm in an emergency—be it fire, equipment failure, or in most cases in the kitchen, an injury to a fellow worker.

The following dishes made up our classical portion of the menu.

Fire! What Fire?
-chapter 19-

Creamed Spinach

Yorkshire Pudding

Potatoes Gratin *(Gratin Dauphinois)*

Prime Rib & Au Jus

JUST THE COOK

The Trials, Tribulations and Recipes from a Catering Chef

MENU RECIPES

WILD MUSHROOM CONSOMMÉ

This wonderful consommé is very easy to make. You can use the very expensive wild mushrooms or the less expensive crimini mushrooms. It is important not to use sea or iodized salt, as they will cloud your consommé.

Yield: 8 six-ounce servings

Ingredients:

32 ounces chicken stock, chilled
2½ cups boiling water
1 ounce cognac, optional
4 ounces dried shiitake mushrooms
8 morels, fresh or dried
1 shallot, peeled
4 fresh shiitake mushrooms, halved
1 pinch white pepper, to taste
kosher salt, to taste

Directions: Place the dried shiitake mushrooms and the morels in a medium-size bowl; add the boiling water and cognac to them. Let the mushrooms stand until they are tender, about 30 minutes, stirring gently now and then. Remove any hard fat from the chilled stock. In a soup pot, add the chicken stock and whole shallot. Remove mushrooms from liquid, reserving liquid. Place soaked mushrooms in soup pot. Gently ladle mushroom liquid from bowl, leaving residue on the bottom of bowl.

Bring consommé to a gentle simmer; add white pepper and salt to taste. Simmer for 30 minutes. Remove morels and place one each in soup bowl; add one shiitake halve to each bowl and ladle in consommé.

AGED SHERRY VINAIGRETTE

When making any vinaigrette, try to use the best vinegar and oils you can afford. Look for sherry vinegar that is aged for at least 8 years and preferably 20 years old. Because the sweetness of vinegars vary, depending on age, it is important that you taste and adjust the sweetness or tartness after blending. If you wish to make less or more vinaigrette, as a general rule make it 1 part vinegar to 3 parts oil.

Yield: 1 cup serves 8 to 12

Ingredients:

⅓ cup aged sherry vinegar
1 medium shallot, finely diced
1 to 2 teaspoons sugar, or to taste
½ teaspoon sea salt, or to taste
⅔ cup extra virgin olive oil

Directions: In a small bowl, add aged sherry vinegar, sugar and salt; whisk until dissolved. Add finely diced shallot; whisk to blend. Slowly add olive oil while whisking. Allow to stand for at least two minutes and whisk again; dip a piece of lettuce in bowl and taste for tartness; adjust salt and pepper. If too tart, add a small amount of sugar; if too sweet, add a small amount of vinegar. This type of vinaigrette will not emulsify.

In a large bowl, pour a small amount of the vinaigrette around the sides of the bowl and place a couple of handfuls of salad greens in bowl; toss gently until all greens are coated and plate salad. Repeat as necessary.

Chef's Note:

This vinaigrette may be done a day ahead of your dinner party.

ROASTED BREAST OF DUCK

I love duck, especially the breast. It's just so versatile; it can be used for either a dinner or lunch entrée, as well as a filling for pasta, or shredded or sliced in a salad. When possible, get the whole duck, have the butcher or yourself remove the breast, legs and thighs, and bring home the carcass for stock.

Yield: 8 servings

Ingredients:
4 whole ducks or 8 duck breasts
kosher or sea salt
black pepper

Directions: Preheat oven to 400 degrees/F. Trim off any excess fat and skin around the duck breasts. Rinse and pat dry. Lightly score across the skin with at least 4 cuts, cutting into the fat but not the flesh. Salt and pepper both sides of the duck.

Heat your sauté pan until hot, but not smoking; add a couple of duck breasts skin side down. Sauté until skin is golden brown. Place browned breasts on a roasting pan skin side up (the breasts can rest until all breasts are browned). Place duck breasts in the preheated oven and roast for 15 minutes for rare or 18 to 20 minutes for medium-rare to medium (well-done will yield a tough breast and not recommended). Remove duck from oven and let rest for 5 minutes before carving. Drain breasts on paper towels before slicing or serving.

Duck Demi-Glace:
To roast the legs, thighs and carcass, place duck parts in a roasting pan, with 1 onion quartered, 2 carrots coarsely chopped, 2 ribs of celery cut into four pieces, and a few

sprigs of thyme. Roast at 400 degrees for about 30 minutes. Remove legs and thighs and reserve. Continue roasting carcass for 15 more minutes. Remove from oven; place carcass and roasted vegetable in a stockpot; cover with cold water and bring to a boil; lower heat to simmer. Skim the scum. After 30 minutes, add 6 whole black peppercorns and the white of a leek. Continue to simmer until stock has reduced to ¼ its original volume. Strain and reserve duck demi-glace for sauces.

Chef's Note:
Serve the roasted legs and thighs or shred and use as a pasta filling.

BING CHERRY SAUCE

This Bing cherry sauce is great with duck. But, it can also be used with ham, roasted pork and Cornish game hens. To change the sauce a little, try using a variety of different dried cherries. If duck demi-glace is not available, you can use 32 ounces of chicken stock (low sodium) reduced to one cup; taste sauce before adding any salt.

Yield: 2 cups sauce

Ingredients:
1 cup duck demi-glace
4 ounces dried Bing cherries
1 cup hot water
1 ounce cognac, optional
2 ounces white wine
1 medium shallot, finely minced
1 sprig fresh thyme
sea or kosher, salt to taste
freshly ground black pepper, to taste

Directions: In a small bowl, add one cup hot water, dried Bing cherries and cognac. Allow cherries to stand for 20 minutes or until cherries are tender. In a saucepan, add white wine and shallots; bring to a boil and reduce to a simmer. Simmer until wine has reduced to a tablespoon. Add duck demi-glace, cherries and the remaining liquid. Heat until simmering; adjust salt and pepper, and serve.

WILD RICE PILAF

I like to use this dish with all types of poultry, both as a side dish or as a stuffing. For a stuffing you can add dried fruits such as apricots, golden raisins or dried cranberries. You may also use various rice, other than white, such as red rice, jasmine rice and brown rice.

Yield: 8 servings

Ingredients:

1 cup wild rice
1 cup long-grain rice
2 cups chicken stock, or water
1 medium shallot, finely diced
1 center of celery with leaves
1 clove garlic, minced
¼ cup olive oil
½ teaspoon lemon zest
sea or kosher salt, to taste
freshly ground black pepper, to taste

Directions: In a saucepan, bring 3 cups of water to a boil. Add the wild rice and a pinch of salt. Stir and bring to a boil; cover and reduce heat to a simmer. Simmer for 35 minutes (wild rice can vary considerably in cooking time). The wild rice should be tender, and the ends popped open. Test for tenderness; drain wild rice and reserve.

In a large heavy saucepan, over medium-high heat, add olive oil and long-grain rice. Stir rice until it turns from opaque to white. Add chicken stock, shallot, garlic, lemon zest, salt and black pepper; stir well. Place the celery stalk on top of rice mixture. (Liquid should cover rice by ¼ inch.) Cover and let simmer on low heat for 20 minutes or until tender. Discard celery stalk. In a large bowl, add wild rice and rice pilaf; fluff and blend with a fork. Cover and keep warm until served.

SAUTÉED PATTYPAN SQUASH

One of the keys to cooking any type of fresh summer squash is heat and quickness. It is essential to use as large of a sauté pan as possible and not to overload it. Overloading causes the squash to steam and not sauté. It's fine to cook the squash in batches. Also, if you wish to serve the squash whole, you can place the squash in salted boiling water for about 3 minutes, then chill in an ice bath, draining before you sauté it.

Yield: 8 servings

Ingredients:
12 green pattypan squash, cut in half tip to bottom
12 yellow pattypan squash, cut in half tip to bottom
1 medium shallot, diced
1 clove garlic, minced
1 whole clove garlic
¼ cup olive oil
1 pat unsalted butter, optional
sea or kosher salt, to taste
freshly ground black pepper, to taste

Directions: In a large sauté pan, over high heat, add olive oil and whole garlic clove. When garlic clove turns a light golden brown, remove from pan. Add pattypan squash (do not overcrowd); add diced shallot, minced garlic, salt and pepper. Stir squash to cook on all sides; sauté until just tender, but not overcooked; add a pat of butter and toss. Remove from heat; the squash will continue to cook after it's removed from heat.

Chef's Note:
For a simple change, squeeze some fresh orange or lemon juice over squash just before removing from heat.

CHAMPAGNE VINAIGRETTE

Just the name of this vinaigrette sounds expensive. However, champagne vinegar is fairly reasonable, and if there is any left over, it makes a wonderful marinade for grilled pork chops or a rack of lamb.

Yield: 8 ounces

Ingredients:

⅓ cup champagne vinegar
1 tablespoon white sugar
1 teaspoon sea or kosher salt, or to taste
1 medium shallot, finely diced
½ teaspoon fresh thyme leaves, chopped
½ teaspoon freshly ground black pepper, or to taste
⅔ cup lite olive oil

Directions: In a medium-sized bowl, add champagne vinegar, sugar and salt. Whisk well, until sugar and salt dissolve. Add diced shallot, chopped thyme leaves and black pepper; slowly add olive oil while whisking. Test taste for sugar and salt with a piece of lettuce.

In a large bowl, pour a small amount of the vinaigrette around the sides of the bowl and place a couple of handfuls of salad greens in bowl; toss gently until all greens are coated and plate salad. Repeat as necessary.

CURRIED ONIONS

This great dish got me out of a jam once, and since then, I have served it with roasted chicken and in an onion tart. Serve the dish over steamed rice, pasta or as a side dish. You can also use leeks; shallots; white, red or yellow onions—in any combination. Another variation is to use either yellow, red or green curry, which changes the heat and flavor all around.

Yield: 8 servings

Ingredients:

6 white onions, halved and sliced thin
1 tablespoon olive oil
1 can unsweetened coconut milk
1 tablespoon yellow curry powder
½ cup heavy cream
white pepper, to taste
sea salt or kosher salt, to taste

Directions: Cut onions in half lengthwise; remove outer skins and slice thin so you get half-moon shaped onion slices. Salt onion slices and reserve. Heat a large Teflon skillet over medium-high heat; add olive oil. Add onions and sauté until onions have become very soft, but not burned. Add curry powder, stirring so it doesn't stick to bottom of pan, adding a little more oil if needed. Spoon out and add only the thick heavy part of the coconut milk to the onions, the heavy cream and white pepper. Turn up heat and bring to a boil; reduce heat to a low simmer and cook for 10 minutes, or until the sauce is thick and coats onions. If thinning is needed, add remaining coconut water from can. Adjust salt and white pepper. Keep warm or serve.

Chef's Note:

Garnish dish with cilantro sprigs and fresh green chile pepper diced finely.

ROASTED BREAST OF CHICKEN
with ORANGE-PINEAPPLE-GIN GLAZE

This is a very simple way to either oven roast or grill great flavor on an otherwise drab chicken breast. This recipe can also be used with pork; just replace the gin with rum or brandy. The alcohol may also be left out of the recipe, but it adds such great flavor. I am a true believer in leaving the bones in when cooking chicken breasts. It adds much more flavor and helps to prevent the breasts from drying out.

Yield: 8 servings

Ingredients:
8 half chicken breasts, bone in, skin on or off
1 cup fresh pineapple purée
1 cup pineapple juice
2 cups fresh orange juice
1 medium shallot, finely minced
1 clove garlic, finely minced
zest of one orange, chopped finely
2 ounces gin
2 teaspoons sugar
sea salt or kosher salt, to taste
freshly ground black pepper

Directions: Preheat oven to 400 degrees. Rinse chicken breasts and pat dry. Remove excess fat and skin if desired. Salt and pepper both sides of chicken. In a mixing bowl, add fresh pineapple, pineapple juice, orange juice, shallot, garlic, orange zest and gin (leave sugar out). Blend well; pour 1 cup of sauce into a small bowl. From small bowl, brush sauce on all sides of chicken and place on a lightly oiled sheet pan. Place remaining sauce in a medium saucepan; add sugar and bring sauce to a boil, then reduce to a simmer. Simmer until sauce has reduced to a glaze; remove from heat. Place chicken breasts in oven on middle rack; roast for 20 minutes or until thermometer reaches 160 degrees or juices run clear. Remove from heat. After the first 15 minutes of roasting, baste the chicken breasts and return to oven. When chicken has reached temperature, remove from oven; baste once more with glaze and serve.

ROASTED BEEF TRI-TIP
with MUSHROOM VODKA SAUCE

This recipe can either be prepared in the oven or on a barbecue. In the mushroom vodka sauce, any type of mushrooms may be used. If desired, the vodka may be omitted or replaced with a brandy or cognac. If you are going to use this sauce with game, I suggest that you use gin as the flavoring agent.

Yield: 8 servings

Ingredients:
4 beef tri-tip steaks
kosher salt
freshly ground black pepper
4 cloves garlic, mashed
¼ cup olive oil
1 pound crimini mushrooms, sliced
1 medium shallot, finely diced
1 clove garlic, minced
3 ounces vodka
2 tablespoons olive oil
1 teaspoon parsley, chopped finely
freshly ground black pepper
sea salt or kosher salt to taste
2 tablespoons unsalted butter, chilled

Directions: Preheat oven to 500 degrees. Rinse tri-tips and pat dry. Trim off any silver skin and excess fat. Rub mashed garlic on all sides of tri-tips. Salt and black pepper tri-tips. In a large heavy skillet, over high heat, add ¼ cup olive oil; heat until almost smoking. Add tri-tips; when well browned on all sides, remove from pan and place on sheet pan, leaving room between them. Place tri-tips on middle rack of oven; reduce to 450 degrees. Roast for 10 to 12 minutes for rare (internal temperature of 125 degrees), 18 to 20 minutes for medium-rare (internal temperature of 140 degrees) in the thickest part of tri-tip. Remove beef from oven and allow meat to rest for at least 5 minutes before carving.

Clean mushrooms by wiping with a damp cloth and slice. In a large hot sauté pan, add the two tablespoons of olive oil, mushrooms, shallots and garlic. Sauté mushrooms until they are tender and their liquid has reduced by half. Add vodka to mushrooms and cook until liquid has reduced by half. Add chopped parsley; taste for salt and pepper and remove from heat; add cold butter and stir with spoon until incorporated and serve.

ASPARAGUS SPEARS
with TOASTED ALMONDS

This is the perfect way to cook asparagus—in the oven! When you steam or boil the asparagus, you leach out flavor (just look at the water). It is very important to peel any spears that are larger than a pencil, not only does it look much more appetizing, but it makes them much more tender. Also trim off the bottoms so they are all the same length. The cooked asparagus may also be chilled after it's cooked and used as a salad, served with your favorite vinaigrette.

Yield: 8 servings, 5 per person

Ingredients:

40 asparagus spears
1 ounce olive oil
2 cloves garlic, crushed
sea or kosher salt
freshly ground black pepper
½ cup almond slivers
1 tablespoon orange zest, chopped

Directions: Preheat oven to 400 degrees. Working in groups, set up asparagus with all of the tips lined up; cut about an inch or more off the bottoms so they are all the same length. With a vegetable or asparagus peeler, peel asparagus to within about ½ inch from bottom of tip. Rinse off the asparagus and let drain (this may be done a day ahead of time, place spears on a damp paper towel in an airtight container and refrigerate).

In a saucepan, heat up olive oil and garlic cloves, just until garlic begins to bubble and turns light brown; remove from heat. Place asparagus spears on a sheet pan with all tips facing the same direction. Pour the cooled garlic-flavored olive oil over spears; sprinkle with the sea salt and freshly ground pepper. Gently toss spears to coat; it is all right to mound them at least 3 to 5 high. Place spears in oven and roast for 8 to 10 minutes, until just tender (do not overcook); pull one out to test the doneness.

In a dry sauté pan, add almond slivers and toss over high heat until they are light golden brown; remove from heat and pan. Allow to cool; sprinkle over asparagus, along with chopped orange zest. Serve asparagus warm.

HERBED RICE PILAF
with PINE NUTS AND GOLDEN RAISINS

I like to use this dish with all types of poultry, both as a side dish or as a stuffing. Like with other stuffings, you can use different dried fruits, such as apricots, dried cranberries or cherries. You may also use various rices, other than white, such as jasmine, brown or red rice. You may also omit the pine nuts or substitute with pecans, hazelnuts or walnuts.

Yield: 8 servings

Ingredients:

1 cup long-grain rice
2 cups chicken stock, or water
1 medium shallot, finely diced
1 clove garlic, minced
¼ cup olive oil
1 center of celery with leaves
1 quarter cup pine nuts
¼ cup golden raisins
sea or kosher salt, to taste
freshly ground black pepper, to taste

Directions: In a large heavy saucepan, over medium-high heat, add olive oil and rice. Stir rice until it turns from opaque to white. Add chicken stock, shallot, garlic, salt and black pepper; stir well. Add pine nuts and golden raisins to the rice. Place the celery stalk on top of rice mixture (liquid should cover rice by ¼ inch). Allow pilaf to come to a boil, cover and let simmer on low heat for 20 minutes or until tender. Discard celery stalk and fluff rice pilaf with a fork. Cover and keep warm until served.

ROASTED FRESH HERB
AND LEMON CHICKEN

This recipe may be used on a whole chicken oven roasted, or in a "set it and forget it" rotisserie oven, even the rotisserie on your propane barbecue works well. Try using this recipe on chicken parts, which are roasted in the oven, or grill on a barbecue. Always try to use chicken with the bones in, as the bones add flavor and help reduce the moisture loss, preventing the chicken from being overdone and dry.

Yield: 8 servings

Ingredients:
8 chicken breasts, skin on, bone in
zest of 2 lemons
2 lemons juiced
2 cloves garlic, finely diced
1 medium shallot, finely diced
1 tablespoon Italian parsley, chopped
1 tablespoon fresh thyme, stemmed and chopped
1 tablespoon fresh rosemary, stemmed and chopped
1 teaspoon sea or kosher salt
freshly ground black pepper
1 tablespoon extra virgin olive oil

Directions: Preheat oven to 400 degrees. Rinse and pat dry chicken breasts; trim away excess fat and skin (leaving skin on). In a mixing bowl, add lemon juice and zest, diced garlic, chopped herbs, salt, black pepper and olive oil. Blend herb mixture very well.

Rub herb mixture over all chicken parts and refrigerate in an airtight container, or plastic bag, for one hour to overnight. If you are using a whole chicken, work your fingers between the skin and flesh on breast, back, legs and thighs. Use a long teaspoon to spoon mixture in pockets between skin and flesh; rub to distribute mixture. Rub remaining herb mixture on outside of chicken and in cavity.

Place chicken on sheet or roasting pan (do not crowd); place in preheated oven. Roast until thermometer reads 160 degrees when inserted into the thickest part of the chicken, about 20 minutes for breasts. When thermometer reaches desired temperature, shut oven off, and let chicken stand for 10 minutes in oven before removing. Collect any juices from sheet pan; bring juices to a boil and serve with chicken. Serve chicken and sauce warm.

GREEN BEAN BUNDLES
WRAPPED with CARROT RIBBONS

This is an easy but decorative way to present green beans as a vegetable. I like to use the French *haricot verts,* or thin green beans. Try using the freshest beans you can get. When at the store or farmer's market, pick one up, snap it for freshness, and taste it. Use carrots that are just a little larger around than a quarter at the top. Don't bother trying to find carrots that have green tops, as the tops pull moisture away from the carrot to stay green, making the carrot a little dryer. Just seek them for firmness and evenness. If the carrot has a root at the tip and it's still crisp, it's a good indicator of freshness.

Yield: 8 servings

Ingredients:

40 + *haricot verts* or green beans, washed
2 8" carrots, peeled
1 medium shallot, finely chopped
1 tablespoon olive oil
1 teaspoon butter or margarine
sea salt or kosher salt, to taste
black pepper, to taste
ice cubes
2 teaspoons salt for water

Directions: In a bowl, add cold water and ice, making an ice bath. Bring water in two saucepans to a boil; add one teaspoon of salt to each. If green beans have fibrous tips, remove them. Trim all beans to the same length if not using *haricot verts*. Place beans in boiling water, and allow to cook until just done, still barely crunchy. Remove from heat; drain and plunge in ice bath; stir gently and remove, placing on paper towel; do not discard ice bath.

Peel carrots. With a vegetable peeler or mandolin, make wide ribbons by peeling down the length of the carrots, making at least 8 and a few extra. Place carrot ribbons in the boiling salted water and boil for just about 30 seconds or until the ribbons are very flexible. Remove from heat; drain and plunge in ice bath. Stir gently and remove, placing on paper towel.

Take 1 carrot ribbon and lay out flat. Place 5 green beans on one end of ribbon and roll firmly but gently until beans are bundled. Repeat until all beans are bundled, placing ends of carrot ribbons down. In a medium-large sauté pan, over medium-high heat, add olive oil and shallots. Sauté until shallots are translucent. Add beans ribbon-end down, butter, and sea salt and black pepper to taste. Gently spoon oil-butter over the top to reheat and serve.

Chef's Note:

A general rule for cooking vegetables is if it grows above ground start them in boiling water; if they grow below ground, start them in cold water. Exception is the carrot ribbons because they are so thin.

TOASTED ORZO with WILD RICE

I love toasted orzo. Because it is a pasta, it always reminds me of my mother's cooking. I have cooked this dish in many different ways; each one of them always turns out great. You can substitute the wild rice with any rice or omit it all together, having just the orzo as your starch. This dish also makes a wonderful stuffing for Cornish hens or duck.

Yield: 8 servings

Ingredients:

1 cup wild rice
1 cup orzo pasta
2 cups chicken stock, or water
1 medium shallot, finely diced
1 center of celery with leaves
1 clove garlic, minced
¼ cup olive oil
sea or kosher salt, to taste
freshly ground black pepper, to taste

Directions: In a heavy saucepan, bring 3 cups of water to a boil. Add the wild rice and a pinch of salt. Stir and bring to a boil; cover and reduce heat to a simmer. Simmer for 35 minutes. (Wild rice can vary considerably in cooking time. The wild rice should be tender and ends popped open.) Drain wild rice and reserve.

In a large heavy saucepan, over medium-high heat, add olive oil and orzo. Stir orzo until it turns from opaque to light golden brown. Add chicken stock, shallot, garlic, salt and black pepper. Stir well. Add celery stalk to top of orzo mixture (liquid should cover orzo by ¼ inch). Stir well and cover, letting simmer on low heat for 20 minutes or until tender. Discard celery stalk.

In a large bowl, add cooked wild rice and cooked orzo; blend and fluff with a fork. Cover and keep warm until served.

MALTED WAFFLES

Waffles are my favorite breakfast food. They can be malted, sourdough, whole wheat, even chocolate, served in just about any fashion. I especially enjoy the Belgian style of waffles, because they're thicker and crispier. The great thing about waffles is that they may be used in other ways. The waffles topping may vary from the usual breakfast toppings to ice cream with sundae syrups or savory flavors may be added to them. They can be cut up and re-toasted in the oven for croutons or chocolate or savory fondues. Both at home and at places where I have worked, we have used F.S. Carbon's "Golden Waffle & Pancake Flour" because it contains malt. The malted waffle mix can be found at a gourmet store or online.

Yield: 8 waffles

Ingredients:
2 whole large eggs
1 cup water
¼ cup milk
1 teaspoon sugar (omit for breakfast or savory waffles)
2 cups Golden Malt Flour
4 tablespoons vegetable oil, or melted butter
2 tablespoons cocoa powder (optional)
spray oil

Dessert Toppings:
1 small basket fresh strawberries, washed and halved
1 basket fresh blackberries
1 small basket fresh raspberries
French vanilla ice cream, softened
powdered sugar (optional)

Directions: In a mixing bowl, beat eggs, water and milk together, then add flour, sugar and cocoa powder; whisk until blended. Stir in oil or melted butter; whisk to remove any lumps. Let batter rest for 5 minutes, or while waffle iron heats up. On hot waffle iron give a light spray of oil and pour in enough batter. Remove when waffles are golden brown and crispy. (Do not stack on each other, as they will get soggy from steam.)

Place a warm waffle on plate; add a scoop of softened ice cream in center and top with various berries. Dust with powdered sugar and serve.

POMEGRANATE VINAIGRETTE

This is about the most colorful vinaigrette you can make. However, it also stains the most, so be careful. Pomegranate juice is now readily available in supermarkets year-round. Try to find one that is pure and unsweetened if possible.

Yield: 1 cup vinaigrette

Ingredients:

1 cup pomegranate juice reduced to ⅓ cup
⅔ cup extra virgin olive oil
1 teaspoon lemon juice (if using sweetened pomegranate juice)
1 medium shallot, finely minced
sea or kosher salt, to taste
freshly ground black pepper, to taste

Directions: In a saucepan, add one cup pomegranate juice and reduce over medium-high heat to ⅓ cup. Let cool. In a medium-sized bowl, add reduced pomegranate juice and salt. Whisk well until salt dissolves. Add diced shallot, freshly ground black pepper; slowly add olive oil while whisking. Test taste for sweetness and salt with a piece of lettuce.

If too sweet, add some lemon juice a little at a time. If too tart, add some sugar or honey and whisk until dissolved.

Chef's Note:

Always test your vinaigrettes with the greens you are serving; some greens may be sweet or bitter, depending on the variety. Adjust flavoring such as salt, acid or sweetness with the greens for a truer flavor. All greens will add moisture, and chewing the greens gives you a full taste in your mouth. If you are using fresh pomegranate seeds as a garnish, taste one to check for sweetness. Also, taste the dressing with the other salad components, just to see how well they all blend together.

ACHIOTE CRUSTED PORK TENDERLOIN

This is an adaptation of a signature dish of mine, Jicarilla Pork. It's named after the Jicarilla Apache Indians of New Mexico, who use the brick-red mud to crust large pieces of meat for roasting in coals of an open fire. Achiote is a spice made from the annatto seed (it's the seed that gives cheddar cheese and butter its yellow color). This may be used on whole pork tenderloin, or as my signature dish with fresh hams or pork shoulders, both cooked with the skin off.

Yield: 8 servings

Ingredients:

3 fresh pork tenderloin, trimmed and silver skin removed
sea or kosher salt
black pepper
3 to 4 tablespoons Achiote condiment (also known
  as annatto)
2 tablespoons olive oil
2 tablespoons tequila
1 teaspoon fresh lemon juice
1 tablespoon kosher salt
1 clove garlic, finely minced

Directions: Preheat oven to 400 degrees. In a large mixing bowl, break up Achiote paste into small pieces; add remaining ingredients. Mix well; it should be a thin paste consistency. Trim excess fat from pork tenderloins; remove any silver skin. Salt and pepper all sides of pork. Place loins in roasting pan; cover meat thoroughly with Achiote mixture. Let meat marinate in refrigerator for 30 minutes. With hands, lightly wipe off excess Achiote mixture; do not rinse. Place loins in oven and roast (or barbecue) for 15 to 20 minutes or until an internal thermometer reads 135 to 140 degrees.

Remove loins from oven and let them for rest five minutes, carry-over heat will continue to cook them. Carefully remove any blackened Achiote crust from the top of the loins, exposing the bright-red wonderful meat. Discard crust. Slice loins and enjoy.

Chef's Note:

If you are using a large cut of meat, decrease the cooking temperature to 350 degrees and increase the amount of cooking time to achieve the proper internal temperature. For full loins or fresh hams, make the paste as thick as you can; do not wipe off and allow crust to blacken before removing from the meat. It acts as a sealant, holding in the juices, revealing a bright red juicy piece of meat; just slice and serve. You can also stud the meat with garlic cloves before roasting.

SPANISH RICE

In southwestern cooking and throughout Mexico, rice is made in a pilaf manner. The rice is lightly sautéed in a vegetable oil or lard, until all the grains have swelled slightly and have turned from white to a light-toasted color. The rice is flavored with various herbs, spices, meats and vegetables. Also along the coasts, they may add seafood. This dish is also known as Mexican Rice.

Yield: 8 servings

Ingredients:

2 cups long-grain rice
½ white onion, small dice
1 clove garlic, minced finely
2 tablespoons tomato paste
½ teaspoon ground cumin
½ teaspoon ground coriander
1 pinch dried oregano, hand crushed
1 celery rib, whole center of stalk with leaves
4 cups chicken or vegetable stock or water
sea or kosher salt, or to taste
3 tablespoons vegetable oil

Directions: In sauté pan with a tight fitting lid, heat pan and add oil and the rice; stir and cook until rice has just begun to brown. Add onion; cook until all of rice has turned light brown; it's all right if a few are a little darker, but not burnt. Add garlic and tomato paste to rice; cook for about one minute; add the stock; stir and add cumin, coriander and hand-rubbed oregano. Place the whole leafy celery rib on top of the rice. Bring to a boil; cover; turn heat to low; simmer for 20 minutes. Uncover; check for doneness; if needed, add ¼ cup of water and continue to cook. Fluff rice with a fork and serve warm.

Chef's Note:

If you are going to add chicken or pork, add the meat in small cubes at the browning phase of the rice. If adding seafood, add it after you place the celery, so not to overcook the seafood.

SAUTÉED CHAYOTE SQUASH

Chayote squash is also known as mirlton, or alligator pears (as is the avocado). It is an avocado-shaped squash that has a very light-green skin. There are two varieties; they either have a smooth skin or a spiny skin. I prefer the smooth-skinned type. Both varieties taste the same, since the difference is that the smooth one comes from a mature plant. There is only one seed, and it's in the center of the vegetable. I think you will enjoy the flavor of this vegetable.

Yield: 8 servings

Ingredients:

3 chayote squash, cubed
1 medium shallot, finely diced
1 clove garlic, minced
2 tablespoons olive oil
black pepper, to taste
sea or kosher salt, to taste
1 pat butter or margarine (optional)

Directions: Cut chayote squash down the center from top to bottom. With a melon baller or a paring knife, remove the small seed from the squash. Dice squash up into ½-inch cubes. In a large sauté pan over medium-high heat, add olive oil and diced chayote. Sauté and stir; after about 1 minute, add the shallot and garlic. Salt and pepper to taste. Continue to sauté until squash is tender. Add a pat of butter or margarine; gently blend and serve.

Chef's Note:

This makes a wonderful stuffed squash because of the shape; just hollow it out and fill it with your favorite stuffing. Bake it in the oven, and because of its firmness, it will hold its shape. In New Orleans, the Cajun call them *piroque,* named after a small pull or pole boat.

TO-DIE-FOR CHOCOLATE MOUSSE

This dessert has been called "to-die-for" and is an easy dessert to make. I have actually had a guest tell me that she'd leave her husband for it. I like this variation of chocolate mousse, because it may be used as a cake filling, and is thick enough to make quenelles or spoonfuls on the side of another dessert. Whipping cream may be added to lighten or extend the mousse, but it also takes away from the rich flavor.

Yield: 8 servings

Ingredients:
18 ounces bittersweet chocolate, finely chopped
1 cup whole milk
1 ounce cognac, optional
3 large eggs yolks, room temperature and beaten
5 large egg whites
4 tablespoons sugar
½ cup heavy whipping cream (optional)

Directions: Melt chocolate over bowl of simmering water (not touching water); once melted remove from heat and place bowl on a towel on the counter until needed. It should still feel warm to touch when used.

Bring milk to boil, then pour over the chocolate. Add cognac, or other flavoring; gently whisk the milk into the chocolate. Add the beaten yolks to chocolate mixture and whisk gently until yolks are fully incorporated. Chill until cool to touch.

In a mixer fitted with whisk attachment, beat egg whites on medium speed just until they hold soft peaks. Increase the speed to medium-high and gradually add the sugar; continue to whisk the whites until they are firm and have slightly stiff peaks, but are still glossy.

Scoop one third of the whites into the chocolate mixture. With a whisk, beat the whites into the chocolate to lighten the mixture. With a rubber spatula, gently fold the remaining whites into the chocolate mixture. Pipe mixture into serving glasses or in large bowl; keep refrigerated in an airtight bowl until served.

Chef's Note:

Whip heavy cream until it reaches stiff peaks; gently fold into mousse for a lighter, fluffier texture. When piping into glasses, do not overfill piping bag, compressing the mousse. The mousse may be made up to one day ahead. However, it will be much heavier; add just a couple of tablespoons of whipped cream to lighten, or serve as is.

Made as a Cappuccino Chocolate Mousse

CAESAR SALAD

Chef Caesar Cardini from Tijuana, Mexico, named this wonderful salad after himself. In the original dressing, there were no anchovies. People confused the Worcestershire sauce with the flavor of anchovies. I like plenty of the salty critters in my dressing. You can always cut back the amount or add more for your taste. The same goes with the amount of lemon juice, since I like my Caesar lemony. Also, never use the grated cheese from a can; freshly grated is all right, but I prefer the shredded and, better yet, shaved Parmesan.

Yield: 8 servings

Ingredients:
1 large whole egg, raw or coddled
8 to 12 small anchovy fillets, packed in oil
1 teaspoon anchovy oil
2 cloves garlic, crushed and minced
¼ cup fresh lemon juice
2 tablespoons red wine vinegar
1 tablespoon Dijon mustard
6 drops Tabasco sauce
1 tablespoon Worcestershire sauce
2 tablespoons Parmesan cheese, shredded or shaved
½ teaspoon sea or kosher salt
black pepper, to taste
1 cup olive oil, not extra virgin
4 hearts of romaine lettuce, cut into 1" pieces
1 cup herbed croutons
Parmesan cheese, as garnish
anchovy fillets, as garnish
lemon zest, optional

Directions: In blender or food processor, add egg, anchovies, anchovy oil, minced garlic, mustard, Tabasco, Worcestershire sauce, ½ the lemon juice, red wine vinegar and lemon zest. Puree; slowly add olive oil to blender with it running to emulsify. Add salt and black pepper to taste; blend well. Taste and adjust lemon and adjust seasoning; add Parmesan cheese.

Remove outer leaves of romaine. Soak leaves in cold water; drain; cut into bite size and spin dry. Mix with lettuce dressing; add garnish of Parmesan, croutons and anchovy fillets on top of salad.

Chef's Note:

This dressing may also be made with whole pasteurized eggs. It can be made up to a day ahead, if kept in the refrigerator.

HERB CRUSTED RACK of LAMB
with ROSEMARY DEMI-GLACE

This is one of my favorite recipes. The crust on the racks may be varied to your tastes, by adding or substituting lemon and mint, black pepper and fine ground coffee, olive Tapénade, even a chile or barbecue rub, all of which add a different twist to the dish. You may also vary the sauce used, or omit it all together and serve a good barbecue sauce instead.

Yield: 8 servings

Ingredients:

4 racks of lamb, frenched
2 large cloves garlic, minced finely
2 tablespoons fresh rosemary, chopped finely
1 tablespoon fresh thyme leaves
kosher salt
black pepper
2 tablespoons lavender vinegar
3 tablespoons rosemary oil or extra virgin olive oil

Directions: Remove fat cap and trim off all excess fat and discard. Remove meat between ribs to ½ inch above loin of rack; scrape bones with paring knife and wipe clean with disposable towel. In a bowl, add chopped garlic, rosemary and thyme; blend well and add salt, black pepper, lavender vinegar and rosemary oil. Rub mixture on lamb meat; cover and let rest at least 20 minutes in refrigerator and up to 24 hours.

Place rack of lamb ribs, bones up, in 400/F degree oven. Roast for 15 to 25 minutes or until internal temperature reaches 135/F for medium-rare. Remove from oven and let rest for 5 to 10 minutes before carving. Collect the carving juices and add to the demi-glace sauce.

ROSEMARY-TRUFFLED DEMI-GLACE SAUCE

Demi-glace can be found either in the frozen department, in the soup and stock section of a specialty food store, or restaurant supply store. If you can't find it, you can try buying some from your favorite restaurant, or make the Quick Demi.

Yield: 1½ cups demi-glace

Ingredients:

1 teaspoon truffle oil
2 shallots, chopped finely
2 whole rosemary sprigs
2 ounces cognac or brandy
1 cup demi-glace or beef stock
kosher salt, to taste
black pepper, to taste
1 teaspoon truffle paste, black or white truffle
3 to 4 ounces cold unsalted butter, cut into pats
meat juices from resting racks

Directions: Heat sauté pan; add truffle oil, shallots and rosemary sprigs; sauté slightly and add cognac; let it come to a boil (it will flame); gently stir sauce to reduce flames. Add demi-glace and meat juices. Remove from heat and add small pieces of butter a little at a time, whisk in, adding more as the butter is almost melted. Add truffle paste; season with salt and black pepper to taste. Keep warm, do not place on direct heat or sauce will break.

Quick Demi:

2 quarts "low sodium" beef stock
2 shallots chopped

1 carrot chopped
1 celery rib chopped
2 potato halves
2 whole black peppercorns

Directions: In a saucepot, add beef stock and vegetables. Bring to a boil and reduce heat to a low simmer. Add the two potato halves (to reduce the saltiness) and simmer the beef stock for one hour; continue to simmer until you have 1½ cups of stock. Strain and continue to simmer down to one cup. Taste for salt. You may have to omit the salt in the sauce if salty.

Chef's Note:

You may omit the rosemary to make it a truffle demi or add morels or wild mushrooms for a fantastic sauce.

DUCHESS POTATOES
POMMES DUCHESSE

Duchess potatoes are an easy-to-make-ahead side dish. The dish goes well with beef Wellington, or any steak dish, and makes an elegant replacement for baked or mashed potatoes. They can be infused with flavors such as garlic, fresh herbs, celeriac or sweet potatoes. This version is garlic infused.

Yield: 8 Duchess Potatoes

Ingredients:

4 large Russet potatoes or Yukon Gold potatoes, peeled and diced large (about 2½ pounds)
salt
1 pinch white pepper
2 grates of fresh nutmeg, or a small pinch of ground nutmeg
3 cloves garlic minced
6 tablespoons unsalted butter
2 large egg yolks
½ cup milk or cream
spray oil
paprika

Directions: Place peeled and large diced potatoes in a 4-quart saucepan with lid; add 1 teaspoon salt and minced garlic; cover with water. Bring to a boil; reduce heat and simmer until tender (about 20 to 25 minutes). Drain potatoes and force through a potato ricer, food mill or mash with a potato masher. Allow potatoes to cool slightly. Taste for salt. Add white pepper, freshly grated nutmeg, butter and milk. Beat in egg yolks one at a time. Cool briefly. At this point, the mixture may be kept in refrigerator overnight.

Preheat oven to 400/F degrees. Spray baking sheet

lightly with oil or line with parchment and spray with oil. Place potato mixture into a large pastry bag, fitted with a large open-star tip, filling the bag only ½ way. Pipe the potatoes into mounds, 2 inches wide at the base and forming a cone 2 inches tall. Spray the potatoes with oil and lightly sprinkle with paprika. Bake until golden brown and crispy (about 15 to 20 minutes).

Chef's Note:

If you would like to reduce the calories in this dish, substitute chicken stock for the cream and low fat yogurt for the butter. However, make sure you check your seasoning. Also, the unbaked leftovers make excellent gnocchi.

ROASTED CARROTS

Who doesn't love roasted root vegetables? It just brings out the sweetness of them along with their caramel color from their sugars. If you don't have the time to fully roast them, you can blanch them until halfway cooked and then pop them in the oven to finish roasting. The pumpkin seed oil is used as a "finishing oil." Drizzle a few drops over the carrots while they are on the serving plate. The oil adds a wonderful dark green color as well as a nutty flavor to the dish. You can find pumpkin seed oil at most health food stores or specialty stores.

Yield: 8 servings

Ingredients:

6 medium-sized carrots
1 medium shallot, finely minced
1 clove garlic, finely chopped
1 tablespoon olive oil
sea or kosher salt, to taste
freshly ground black pepper, to taste
1 tablespoon pumpkin seed oil, for garnish

Directions: Preheat oven to 400 degrees. Peel carrots, yes, even the whole baby carrots with the exception of the processed baby carrots. Cut the carrots into desired serving sizes. In a small roasting pan, add carrots, shallots, garlic, oil, salt and pepper. Toss to coat evenly. Place in oven and roast for approximately 15 to 20 minutes, or until tender. Remove from oven and drizzle pumpkin seed oil over the top of the plated carrots.

Chef's Note:

You can easily make maple-glazed carrots as a holiday treat, by drizzling a couple of tablespoons of maple syrup over them a few minutes before serving.

Pumpkin seed oil available at www.arnabal.com.

RÉMY CRÈME

This cream is really very simple to make. It is based on the classical dessert sauce, *Créme Anglaisé,* also known as a French custard sauce. You may replace the Rémy Martin Cognac with your favorite brand, or just about any flavoring, alcoholic or otherwise—flavorings such as mint, chocolate, hazelnut, melon, raspberry, and cherry, all of which can be used on various desserts. Once you have the method down, just change the ingredients. It is important not to overheat the sauce, or you will scramble the yolks.

Yield: 1½ cups sauce

Ingredients:

3 large egg yolks
1¼ cups hot milk
⅓ cup granulated sugar
1 vanilla bean, split
  or 2 teaspoons vanilla extract
1 tablespoon Rémy Martin Cognac

Directions: With a wooden spoon, beat the yolks in a saucepan until they are sticky; add the granulated sugar and continue to beat. Then, add a few drops of hot milk while stirring with the wooden spoon, mixing well. Continue slowly adding the hot milk, a small amount at a time, while stirring the egg mixture. Place the saucepan over medium-low heat; add the split vanilla bean, slowly stirring the sauce constantly until sauce thickens enough to coat the spoon. Do not let the heat of the sauce come near simmer or the yolks will curdle.

Remove from heat; add the cognac or other flavoring and the extract, if not using whole vanilla bean. Serve warm or cold.

Chef's Note:

For a thicker cream, replace the milk with heavy cream. Place the sauce in a squeeze bottle for more efficient saucing. If not using warm, seal in airtight container and keep refrigerated for up to two days. If you need this sauce in a hurry, just melt some French vanilla ice cream and add the cognac. It's not quite the same, but works in a pinch. We've all used it as an emergency fix.

SHORTCAKE

Dessert shortcakes are nothing more than breakfast biscuits with sugar and vanilla added. Please don't use the hollowed-out sponge bread they sell in the supermarkets. If you need a quick dessert and don't have time to make the shortcakes, use pound cake. You can use any type of fresh sweet berry in this dish. Life is much more than just strawberries. Try gooseberries, blackberries, blueberries and even kiwi, papaya or mango for a tropical treat.

Yield: 12 shortcakes

Ingredients:

4 cups all-purpose flour
8 tablespoons granulated sugar
1 teaspoon vanilla
1 tablespoon baking powder
2 cubes (8 ounces) unsalted butter, cut into ½-inch cubes, chilled
½ teaspoon salt
1 cup plus 2 tablespoons half & half or whole milk
2 large eggs, lightly beaten
1 large egg white, lightly beaten

Berries

3 baskets ripe berries
2 tablespoons fine sugar
1 tablespoon cognac

Directions: Place oven rack in lower-middle position; preheat oven to 425 degrees. In a food processor bowl, add flour, 5 tablespoons of the granulated sugar, baking powder and salt. Pulse to blend. Add the butter pieces around the bowl and pulse about 15 to 18 times until it resembles coarse sand; transfer to a bowl. In a small bowl, add lightly beaten whole eggs, vanilla and half & half; blend well. Add egg mixture to flour mixture. Combine with a rubber spatula until large clumps form.

Turn dough onto a lightly floured surface; gently knead dough until it just comes together. Gently shape into two 9 x 6 rectangles about ¾-inch thick (dough may be covered with plastic and refrigerated for up to two hours). Flour a 2¾-inch or 3-inch round cutter or water glass to make 6 cutouts. Repeat with other rectangle. Place discs 1 inch apart on a greased baking sheet. Brush shortcake biscuit tops with beaten egg white and sprinkle the remaining sugar. Place in the oven, for about 10 to 12 minutes or until puffed and lightly brown. Allow to cool on a rack; cut or pull apart at natural crack and keep matching halves together.

In a small mixing bowl, add about half of the berries and mash; slice remaining strawberries; add sugar and cognac; let berries macerate for up to two hours. Place shortcake bottom on plate; add some of the berries to it; top with cream sauce; place shortcake top on top of cream sauce and top again with berries and a little of the juice; top with whipped cream. Add whole berry garnish on top. Add a little cream sauce to the plate as a garnish.

GREEN PAPAYA SALAD

This Thai salad is known as *Som Tum Thai.* It is a favorite of the Thai people, who love the juxtaposition of the hot from the chile peppers and the coolness from the papaya. You can use as many peppers as you like. If you aren't really tolerant of the chiles, just use a milder jalapeño or yellow wax, and then just the flesh, not the seeds. This salad is actually great as a side dish for your outdoor barbecues. It brings new flavors to old favorites. If you live near an Asian market*, they may have pre-shredded green papaya and palm sugar. If not, look for the hardest-green ones you can find. And no matter how much you make, you won't have enough!

Yield: 8 servings

Ingredients:

2 tablespoon palm sugar* or light brown sugar or raw sugar
3 limes, juiced
6 cups shredded green papaya*
    or 4 medium green papaya, shredded
1 large clove garlic, crushed
2½ tablespoons fish sauce (*nam pla*)*
2 tablespoons baby dried shrimp*
4 Thai chiles, seeded and stemmed*
8 cherry tomatoes, halved
16 green beans, blanched and chilled
2 tablespoons roasted peanuts
shredded cabbage

Directions: Blanch green beans in salted water until just done. They should still have a little crunch; remove from water; drain and plunge in an ice bath to arrest cooking. Shred a peeled papaya with cheese grater, or used pre-shredded papaya; place in a large bowl and set aside.

In a mortar, add the garlic and crush it; add the tomatoes, palm sugar, fish sauce and lime juice, crushing and blending well with the pestle. Add the baby dried shrimp and crush with pestle. Add the chile flesh and crush with pestle. Smash up ingredients very well and add the green beans, just bruising them, allowing some of the flavors to enter them. Place mixture in bowl with papaya and toss gently to coat. Cover and chill or serve immediately.

To serve, place shredded cabbage or whole leaf on a plate and add papaya salad on top. Garnish with roasted peanuts on the top.

Chef's Note:

If you don't have a mortar and pestle, place ingredients in food processor or blender (except for papaya) and purée. This may be done a day before and add to the papaya just before serving.

The best way to remove the chile flesh from the veins and seeds is by slightly cutting off the tip of the chile. With your free hand (the other is holding the knife), hold the stem of the chile; place the flat, cut tip on the cutting board, and slice down from the shoulder to the tip of the chile. You should be able to see the veins and cut between the veins and flesh, leaving the core, seeds and veins attached to the stem, discard. Then, turn the chile slice, skin side down and slice it lengthwise into strips; turn and cut strips into very small dices, or just process the chile strips.

SHRIMP AND CILANTRO SOUP
with FRESH THAI CHILE PEPPERS

This Thai soup is called *Dom Yam Gung*. This is a very simple soup to make and goes great with any Asian dinner.

Yield: 8 servings

Ingredients:

6 whole peppercorns
6 lemon grass stalks, cut into ¼-inch rings
6 slices *galangal* or young ginger
⅓ cup fresh lime juice
4 red Thai chiles, seeded and finely diced
12 cilantro stems
4 cups clam juice
4 cups shrimp stock
24 medium-large shrimp, uncooked with shells
5 tablespoons fish sauce (*nam pla*)
4 tablespoons chopped cilantro leaves

Directions: Peel and devein shrimp, reserving the shells. Cut root end of lemon grass and discard outer leaves. Cut the more tender part of lemon grass stalk into ¼-inch rings. In a medium pot, add 5 cups cold water, whole peppercorns, lemon grass rings, cilantro stems, ginger slices and shrimp shells. Bring shrimp stock to a boil and reduce heat to a simmer; simmer uncovered for 20 minutes or until stock has reduced to about 4 cups. Strain, discard solids, reserving shrimp stock. Bring shrimp stock to a boil, adding water if needed to make 4 cups. Skim off any scum from stock. Reduce heat to a simmer; add clam juice, lime juice, fish sauce and peeled shrimp. When shrimp have turned to a bright pink or red, remove from heat and serve, dividing shrimp to 3 per bowl. Garnish soup with diced chile and cilantro leaves.

Chef's Note:

The easiest way to clean and devein shrimp is with scissors. Place the tip of one side of the scissors in the center of the shrimp and cut to the tail; remove vein with thumbnail and peel shell off.

CHICKEN IN GREEN CURRY

This Thai curry stew is very popular. The chicken may be replaced with any seafood or meat, depending on what is available. This dish is almost always served over, or with, plain or jasmine rice.

Yield: 8 servings

Ingredients:

6½ chicken breasts, skinless & boneless cut
  into 1-inch cubes
4 cans unsweetened coconut milk, unshaken
coconut cream from coconut milk
6 slices galangal or young ginger
2 stalks lemon grass, chopped finely
4 tablespoons fish sauce (*nam pla*)
3 tablespoons Thai green curry paste
8 kaffir lime leaves, dried or frozen
¾ cup Thai basil leaves, or green basil
4 green Thai chiles or green serrano chiles, stemmed
  and seeded
1 cup small Thai eggplants or green peas
1 cup chicken stock or water
1 recipe Coconut Jasmine Rice

Directions: Cut the chicken breasts into 1-inch cubes and reserve. Open coconut milk cans and spoon off and reserve the thick coconut cream from milk. If the cream and milk have not separated, let stand for an hour. Cut the root end off the lemon grass, remove the tough outer leaves and chop the tender white part of lemon grass. Cut stemmed and seeded chiles into strips.

In a wok or saucepan, add the thick coconut cream, galangal, lemon grass and fish sauce. Cook over high heat until sauce becomes thick and oily. Add the green curry paste; stir well and cook for about 2 minutes, stirring frequently. Reduce heat to medium; add chicken and stir. Cook chicken for about 2 minutes. Add remaining 2 cups of thin coconut milk, the kaffir lime leaves, ½ cup of the basil leaves, chile strips and Thai eggplant or peas. Bring back to a boil, stirring frequently, and simmer for 5 minutes. If sauce is too thick, thin with chicken stock or water. Serve with jasmine rice and garnish with the remaining Thai basil leaves.

Chef's Note:

Thai eggplant are just a little bit bigger than green peas; if Thai eggplants are not available, peas make a fine substitute. You may replace the kaffir lime leaves with fresh citrus leaves, or lime skin or zest, no pith; however, it's not quite the same. The amount of heat is adjustable by the amount of chiles added.

COCONUT JASMINE RICE

For this dish, I like using a rice cooker, since they are almost foolproof. You may substitute the jasmine rice with any medium or long-grain rice.

Yield: 8 servings

Ingredients:

4 cups water
2 cups uncooked jasmine rice
½ teaspoon sea or kosher salt
½ cup unsweetened shredded coconut

Directions: In the rice cooking pot or in a small pot, add rice and fill halfway up with water; stir rice vigorously; drain water and repeat three times. Add 4 cups of water to drained rice; add shredded coconut and salt. Place back in rice cooker; replace lid and turn on.

Or, add 4 cups of water to rice, shredded coconut and salt in a small pot with a tight fitting lid. Add shredded coconut and salt to rice; bring water to a rapid boil. Stir and reduce heat to low; cover and let simmer for 15 to 18 minutes.

When rice cooker or timer dings, fluff rice with a fork and serve.

GINGERED BABY BOK CHOY

The tender bright-green color and crunchiness of the baby bok choy makes this a great vegetable side dish for many other entrées, such as fish or chicken.

Yield: 8 servings

Ingredients:
4 to 8 baby bok choy, depending on size
2 tablespoons chopped galangal or young ginger
1 teaspoon chopped garlic
1 teaspoon sesame seed oil
1 teaspoon vegetable oil
sea or kosher salt, to taste
1 teaspoon lemon juice

Directions: Plunge bok choy in a large bowl of water and shake them to remove any sand or dirt. Remove from water and drain upside down. With the tip of the knife, pierce the thicker part of stalks of the bok choy. If the base or bunches of the stalks are thick, cut bunches in half lengthwise for even cooking. In a wok or large sauté pan, over medium-high heat, add vegetable oil and bok choy; then add the chopped garlic, galangal and salt; sauté until greens are tender and white parts are just turning tender. Add sesame seed oil and lemon juice; coat and serve.

COCONUT GINGER ICE CREAM

Homemade ice cream is great because you can make any flavor you like. Making ice cream at home has become so easy with the modern ice cream makers, which have the inserts you freeze, instead of the noisy churned types requiring ice and salt. This recipe should fit in most home ice cream makers.

Yield: 1 batch

Ingredients:
2 whole eggs
⅔ cup sugar
1¾ cup whole milk
2 cups heavy cream
1 teaspoon vanilla extract
¼ cup coconut cream, from coconut milk (unshaken)
1 tablespoon fresh ginger juice
2 tablespoons candied ginger, finely diced

Directions: Follow manufacturer's instructions on freezing container. Open the unshaken can of coconut milk; carefully remove the heavy coconut from the top of the can and reserve. Grate fresh ginger and squeeze grated ginger to extract only the juice; discard pulp.

Beat eggs and milk together in the top portion of a double boiler; add sugar and cook in double boiler over medium heat, stirring constantly. Do not overheat or allow water to touch bottom of top pot, or eggs will curdle. Cook until mixture thickens, about ten minutes. The egg mixture should coat the back of a spoon. Remove from heat and cool mixture completely in an ice bath. (Note: if using a glass double boiler, transfer to a metal bowl to cool.) Add heavy cream and coconut cream. (Mixture may be refrigerated overnight at this point.) Place coconut mixture in ice cream maker and follow manufacturer's run time. Remove from ice cream maker, fold in candied ginger, and serve or place in airtight container in freezer.

Chef's Note:

This is your basic ice cream recipe. To change the flavor, just omit the coconut cream and candied ginger, adding additional flavor(s) when you add the heavy cream and fresh fruit at the end.

SOURDOUGH CROUTONS

I just can't believe that people buy pre-made croutons. They are so easy to make and so much tastier than pre-made. How many times have you tossed out that half loaf of sourdough bread? It's just calling out for a little olive oil and herbs.

Yield: 1 cup croutons

Ingredients:

1½ cup sourdough cubes, fresh or slightly stale
¼ cup olive oil
1 tablespoon finely chopped parsley
1 teaspoon finely chopped garlic
1 teaspoon finely chopped thyme
1 teaspoon finely chopped rosemary
1 teaspoon kosher salt
½ teaspoon freshly ground black pepper

Directions: Preheat oven to 300 degrees. Cut the crust off the bread, cut bread into ½- to ¾-inch cubes. In a mixing bowl, add oil, chopped herbs, salt and black pepper; blend well. Toss cubes in herb mixture, making sure they are fully coated. Lay out seasoned bread cubes on a cookie sheet and bake for 10 to 15 minutes or until just slightly golden. Remove from oven and allow to cool before using.

Chef's Note:

Other herbs and seasonings can be used, such as paprika, dill, ground cumin, coriander, Cajun or creole seasoning, lemon zest, orange zest, garlic powder, onion powder and sage. It's a good way to clean out those old spices. You can also use different oils, such as garlic oil, rosemary oil, walnut or hazelnut oil and butter. If you are going to use the croutons as a stuffing, you may either toast them or use the seasoned soft bread cubes.

BEEF WELLINGTON

This is a classic and wonderfully easy dish to make. Serve it to celebrate an event while impressing the heck out of your guests. The better the mushrooms are, the tastier your Wellingtons will be. Serve along with Duchess or mashed potatoes.

Yield: 8 individual Beef Wellingtons

Ingredients:
8 4-6 ounce beef fillets, fillet mignons
1 package of puff pastry dough
1 pound mushrooms, finely minced
2 shallots, finely minced
2 ounces cognac or brandy
2 tablespoons olive oil
¼ pound butter, unsalted (one cube, cut into pats)
black pepper, to taste
kosher salt, to taste
1 whole egg, whisked for egg wash
truffle oil, optional
1 cup beef demi-glace reduction or mix

Directions: Remove puff pastry from freezer; remove from packaging cover and allow to thaw to room temperature. Lightly oil, salt and pepper both sides of steaks. Heat a heavy pan over high heat for three minutes. When it's hot, add the beef and brown on one side for 1 minute and turn over and brown another minute. Remove and let cool.

To make Duxelle: In food processor, add mushrooms and chop until finely minced; it should look like coarse sand. Hand chop or process shallots until very fine. In sauté pan over medium-high heat, add butter, and when melted, add mushrooms, pinch of salt and a few grinds of black pepper;

sauté until most of the moisture has evaporated; remove from heat; add cognac; stir and place back on heat. Continue to cook until almost all moisture has evaporated. Allow duxelle mixture to cool.

Take one layer of thawed puff pastry and gently unfold. Gently fold creases down and overlap any cracks in creases. With pizza cutter or knife, cut into quarters. Dust a flat rolling surface with flour and roll out each quarter one at a time. Gently brush off any excess flour and cover.

Preheat oven to 400 degrees. Pat dry each cooled fillet; then place a heaping tablespoon of duxelle on each fillet and spread evenly on the top, adding more if needed. Place the fillet, duxelle-top down, on a rolled-out puff quarter. Lightly brush ½ inch of egg wash on top surface edges to act as glue. Fold pastry dough over fillet covering, sealing bottom. Turn Wellington over and set on sheet pan; gently round and form with the palms of your hands. Repeat until all Wellingtons are done. Brush tops and side of Wellington with a light coat of egg wash. With a sharp paring knife, gently cut two or three small 1-inch slits in tops of Wellingtons, opening slits gently. Place in oven and lower heat to 350 degrees. Bake for about 15 to 20 minutes or until the puff pastry is golden brown.

Make or reheat demi-glace or brown sauce to serve with Wellington. After Wellingtons are removed from oven, I suggest drizzling a few drops of truffle oil into the cut slots. Plate Wellingtons and spoon sauce around them, not on top.

RED POTATOES
with ROSEMARY AND GARLIC

This recipe calls for *tourner* or turned potatoes, which is a classically French way of presenting them. Each potato is cut into the shape of a 2-inch long football with 7 equal sides. However, a much simpler way is by using baby red or Yukon gold potatoes, taking your vegetable peeler and peeling a strip around the equator of the potato. The potatoes may also be left whole. You may also replace the rosemary with parsley or thyme, almost any fresh herb to suit the dish.

Yield: 8 servings

Ingredients:

24 new or baby red potatoes
¼ cup olive oil
6 cloves garlic, crushed
6 fresh rosemary stems
sea or kosher salt, to taste
freshly ground black pepper

Directions: Rinse potatoes and let dry. Preheat oven to 400 degrees. In a large bowl, add olive oil, garlic, salt and black pepper. Mix well; add potatoes and coat evenly. Place rosemary stems on the bottom of sheet pan. Place potatoes on top and place in oven. Bake for 20 to 30 minutes or until tender and golden. Discard rosemary and serve.

Chef's Note:

In restaurants, we always make extras, so we have the cooked potatoes for home fries or potato salad. We also use flavored oils such as garlic oil, rosemary oil, basil oil and walnut oil. Make sure you use waxy potatoes such as Yukon Gold, White or Fingerlings, not the starchy Russets.

BROCCOLI FLORETS
with ORANGE HOLLANDAISE

If you love broccoli, you'll love this dish. Of course, the orange hollandaise doesn't hurt. You can use nice green, tight, broccoli florets or buds with short stems; broccolini; Brussels sprouts; cauliflower; even artichokes. For home use, I peel the stems and cook them a little longer until tender. The hollandaise is a simple one to make.

Yield: 8 servings, about 1½ cups sauce

Ingredients:

3 heads fresh broccoli
1 medium shallot, finely diced
3 large egg yolks
2 tablespoons concentrated orange juice, undiluted
1 teaspoon orange zest, finely minced
1 pinch sea or kosher salt
½ pound (2 cubes) unsalted butter, cut into pats
1 small pinch cayenne pepper
white pepper, to taste

Directions: Cut florets away from broccoli core, leaving about ½ stem on them. If you prefer, peel, core and slice into bite-size pieces. In a medium-large bowl, add cold water and ice. In a saucepot, bring lightly salted water to a boil. Add florets and simmer until just tender; drain and plunge into ice bath to stop cooking process. When completely cooled, remove and drain (this may be done up to a day ahead).

For the Hollandaise: Whisk the egg yolks, orange zest and the orange juice concentrate together in a heavy saucepan on the top of a double boiler. Add a pinch of salt and whisk until sauce is thick and creamy.

Set the saucepan over very low heat, or over

simmering water in the lower pan of the double boiler, and begin whisking immediately. Continue to whisk until the egg mixture just begins to thicken; the wires of the whisk should begin to leave tracks in the sauce, in which you can see the bottom of the pan. Remove the pan from heat and slowly add one pat of butter at a time while continually whisking, adding another pat of butter as each begins to melt. When all of the butter is incorporated, add the cayenne and white pepper. Taste and adjust the salt. Serve immediately or cover and keep warm, but not hot or over direct heat for up to 30 minutes.

In a sauté pan over medium-high heat, add a pat of butter and diced shallots. When shallots have turned translucent, add broccoli florets and sauté just to heat up. Serve broccoli on plates and ladle the orange hollandaise over it.

Chef's Note:

By using whole butter, you add the water contained in the butter, which helps to emulsify the sauce and helps to keep it from breaking.

FRESH STRAWBERRIES IN KIRSCH
with VANILLA AND MASCARPONE CREAM

I love berries that have been macerated in a liquor. Of course, you can use just about any type of berry. If they are out of season, don't be afraid of the Individually Quick Frozen (IQF) berries, since they are picked at their peak and frozen. Thawed slowly in the refrigerator, they are usually sweeter than fresh market berries. You may omit the Mascarpone Cheese, to shave off a few calories.

Yield: 8 servings, 4 cups berries

Ingredients:
4 cups strawberries
1 cup kirsch or other liquor
2 tablespoons sugar
½ teaspoon salt
1 cup heavy cream, chilled
1 teaspoon vanilla extract
2 teaspoons sugar
6 ounces Mascarpone cheese

Directions: In a large bowl filled with cold water, place strawberries (except frozen) and gently toss to remove dirt and excess seeds. Let berries drain; hull berries. Cut a portion of the berries in half or quarters and place cut and whole berries in a bowl; add kirsch and 2 tablespoons of sugar. Toss berries gently and let macerate for at least 15 minutes, up to one hour, gently tossing every so often, so all the berries are coated.

In a mixing bowl, add the chilled heavy cream, vanilla extract and 2 teaspoons sugar. Whisk or whip to stiff peak. Gently fold in the Mascarpone cheese; do not overwork or Mascarpone will break beyond repair (I've done this more than once).

Drain berries (reserving liquor). Place some berries in compote bowls; spoon a teaspoon or two over berries. Top with Mascarpone cream; garnish with a whole strawberry.

CROSTINI

This is the base for many different types of appetizers. You may cut the bread (preferably a baguette) across into rounds or on the bias for longer pieces. The type of oil or butter may vary with your needs. I like using either all butter or an olive oil-butter combination. But, flavored oils are also wonderful to use. The toppings can really vary, from sliced egg to pâté. The only boundary is your imagination and access to ingredients. These also make great croutons and soup crackers.

Yield: 24 crostini

Ingredients:

1 baguette, sweet or sour
3 tablespoons unsalted butter
1 clove garlic, crushed
½ cup olive oil

Directions: Preheat oven to 250 degrees. Slice baguette across into 24 rounds about ⅛-inch thick. If there are rounds with large holes in them, discard or set aside if you have enough rounds.

In a saucepot, melt butter with oil and crushed garlic; do not boil. Once butter has melted, remove from heat. Place rounds on a sheet pan. With a pastry brush, lightly brush the tops of the baguette rounds. Place sheet pan in oven and bake for 15 to 20 minutes or until just toasted, slightly golden (not brown). Allow crostini to cool. Once crostini have completely cooled, over an hour, they may be placed in an airtight container for up to 4 days.

Chef's Note:

You may change the types of oils used or bump up the garlic. Add fresh herbs or salt and pepper if you are going to use them as a crouton or cracker.

SPANISH OLIVE TAPÉNADE

For this dish, you can easily substitute your favorite olives. I love using black Spanish olives or green olives, depending on my mood. You may also use sun-dried tomatoes, roasted red peppers, artichoke hearts and roasted garlic in place of or added to the olives.

Yield: one cup

Ingredients:
1 12-ounce can pitted black olives
6 pimento-filled olives
4 anchovy fillets, packed in oil
1 clove garlic
2 tablespoons chopped parsley
2 tablespoons extra virgin olive oil
black pepper, to taste
salt, to taste

Directions: In a food processor, add all of the ingredients, except for salt, and purée into a coarse paste. Taste and adjust salt; if too dry, add a little more olive oil. Excess tapénade may be kept in refrigerator for up to 3 days.

I like going to a deli and getting several types of olives for a more exotic blend of flavors.

PAELLA VALENCIANA

The word Paella is the name for the shallow two-handled pan. Other types of ingredients may also be used in this dish, such as rabbit or duck, pork, fish, clams, squid or lobster.

Yield: 8 servings

Ingredients:
8 chicken legs with thighs, separated
2 links Spanish chorizo, sliced on a bias
16 mussels, remove beards just before cooking
24 prawns, peeled & deveined, tails on
8 diver scallops, side muscle removed
4 Roma tomatoes, peeled, seeded and chopped
1 medium yellow onion, diced finely
4 cloves garlic, minced finely
1 pimento, roasted and sliced
½ teaspoon saffron threads, crushed
8 ounces green peas, fresh or frozen
2 cups arborio rice
2 cups chicken stock
2 cups water
1 tablespoon parsley, chopped
2 teaspoons kosher salt
1 lemon, quartered
bay leaf
½ cup olive oil

Directions: Separate chicken thighs from legs; rinse and pat dry. In the paella pan or large sauté pan, add olive oil over medium-high heat. Add chicken and fry until a little over half done; remove from pan; add sliced chorizo; brown lightly; remove and drain.

Add rice to hot oil and sauté, stirring until it changes color to white; add diced yellow onion; sauté until translucent. To rice, add saffron threads, sauté lightly; add water, chicken stock, salt, garlic, tomatoes and bay leaf; stir gently. Arrange chicken, chorizo, lemon wedges and seafood on top of rice with mussels facing up. Sprinkle green peas and pimento over rice; bring liquid to a boil; reduce heat to simmer and cover rice.

Cook paella until mussels are open. The shrimps and scallops should turn from translucent to opaque and the rice is tender, adding a little water if needed. Let paella stand uncovered for 5 minutes before serving, discarding any mussels that did not open; sprinkle chopped parsley over the top.

Chef's Note:

This is a party dish, so have one!

PUMPKIN SOUP
with TOASTED PUMPKIN SEEDS

This soup can be made with either fresh pumpkin or from the can. When you use fresh pumpkin, cut it up into manageable pieces and place it in a pot with a lid. Place about 2 inches of water in the pan and bring to a boil. Simmer until pumpkin is cooked; let cool. Remove pulp from skin with large spoon and purée in processor. This purée can be used for pumpkin pies or soup, or cooked with a little salt and butter as a vegetable. After all, pumpkins can be used for much more than jack-o-lanterns.

Yield: 10 6-ounce servings

Ingredients:

1 can (58 ounces) pumpkin purée, canned pumpkin
1 quart (64 ounces) chicken stock, low sodium
4 ounces (½ cup) heavy cream
1 tablespoon grated ginger juice
½ teaspoon ground cloves
½ teaspoon ground cinnamon
½ teaspoon white ground pepper
2 teaspoons kosher salt, or to taste

Garnish:

½ cup peeled raw pumpkin seeds, toasted
pumpkin seed oil, optional
1 cup sour cream, optional
2 tablespoons brown sugar, optional
Ginger Snap Cookies

Directions: In large pot, add chicken stock and pumpkin purée; bring to a boil; then reduce to a simmer; skim foam from top. Add cloves, cinnamon, ginger juice and white pepper. Let soup simmer for 20 minutes. Reduce heat and add cream; continue to simmer for 15 minutes or until desired thickness; add salt to taste.

Toast pumpkin seeds until slightly brown; do not burn. Add a few of the toasted pumpkin seeds on the top of each bowl and a few drops of pumpkin seed oil.

Or, mix the brown sugar with the sour cream and add a dollop on top of the bowl of soup and garnish with a few pumpkin seeds; place a gingersnap cookie on each plate.

Chef's Note:

Homemade gingersnap cookies can be made. Shape them like crackers and use a little less sugar in them.

RASPBERRY VINAIGRETTE

This vinaigrette is great on baby greens or arugula. The sweetness helps tame the pepperiness of arugula or bitter greens. There are hundreds of versions of this dressing. This dressing is my favorite.

Yield: 2 cups vinaigrette

Ingredients:

½ cup raspberry vinegar
¼ cup balsamic vinegar
½ cup raspberry jam
1 medium shallot, minced
¾ cup olive oil
freshly ground black pepper, to taste
sea or kosher salt, to taste

Directions: In a mixing bowl or food processor, add raspberry vinegar, balsamic vinegar, raspberry jam and minced shallot. Process or whisk to emulsify. Slowly add olive oil to emulsify. Add salt and black pepper to taste. Test taste with a piece of lettuce to check sweetness. If too sweet, add more raspberry vinegar; if too tart, add a little more jam. This vinaigrette will keep for up to one week refrigerated.

Chef's Note:

You may omit the balsamic vinegar; replace with raspberry vinegar. Or you may use just balsamic vinegar, but the dressing tends to be on the sweet side. This also makes a great marinade for chicken.

If you don't want the seeds in the vinaigrette, just strain the raspberry vinegar, balsamic and raspberry jam, before adding the chopped shallots.

VEAL PICCATA

This magnificent dish gets its name from the tartness of the lemon and capers. Make sure that your butcher gives you veal from the "top round" and cut the veal against the grain. This cut of meat can also be called scallopini. You may use different types of breading. I prefer either seasoned flour or panko breadcrumbs for a crispier crust.

Yield: 8 servings

Ingredients:
2 pounds veal scallopini, 8 cutlets, pounded to ¼-inch thick
2 cups all-purpose flour
1 teaspoon kosher salt
1 teaspoon freshly ground black pepper
3 to 4 tablespoons olive oil
½ cup unsalted butter, 1 stick cut into pats
½ cup chopped shallots
1 cup white wine
4 tablespoons lemon juice
½ cup veal stock or low sodium beef stock
3 tablespoons drained capers
8 lemon wedges
2 tablespoons chopped parsley

Directions: Place the veal between two pieces of wax paper or plastic and pound the steaks to ¼-inch thickness. In a bowl, mix flour, salt and black pepper. Working in small batches, dredge as many pieces of veal that will very loosely fit in a large sauté pan. Place the sauté pan over medium-high heat; add 1 tablespoon of olive oil and a pat or two of butter. When melted butter begins to bubble, add floured veal and sauté until golden brown on one side; turn over and continue to sauté until done. Remove browned veal and reserve, keeping warm.

To the hot sauté pan, add some chopped shallots, a little white wine, some lemon juice and some veal stock to deglaze the pan. Make sure you scrape the bottom of the pan to get all of the tasty brown pieces. Place and reserve the sauce in another sauté pan. Repeat process until all of the veal is sautéed.

Heat up reserved sauce in the sauté pan; bring to a boil; add capers; adjust seasoning and turn heat off. Add butter a little at a time, shaking the sauté pan or whisking it into the sauce, until all of the butter is melted. Place veal on plate; spoon some sauce over the top of each and garnish with chopped parsley and a lemon wedge.

Chef's Note:

You can change the recipe by adding sun-dried tomatoes, a few green olives, even mushrooms. You may also replace the wine with malt vinegar, champagne or balsamic vinegar. I suggest the addition of a good Pinot Noir to go with this dish.

SOUTHERN BLUE CRAB CAKES

This crab cake recipe can by used with any type of crab, shrimp or fish. I often make salmon cakes and have even used the Surimi Crab for those with shellfish allergies. If you have fish in the freezer and it feels a little mushy when thawed, why not make fish cakes? Just chop up or lightly purée.

Yield: approximately 25 1½" crab cakes

Ingredients:

3 large eggs
2 cups panko breadcrumbs
2 tablespoons celery, finely minced
1 tablespoon shallot, finely minced
2 tablespoons Old Bay seasoning
1 teaspoon fresh or dried dill
1 pinch of black pepper
1 teaspoon sea or kosher salt
1 cup mayonnaise, unsweetened
1 lemon zested, chopped finely
1 lemon, juiced
1 pound blue crab, lump meat, drained
oil to sauté crab cakes

Directions: In a large bowl, except for crab, mix all ingredients together and blend well. Add crabmeat and toss gently. The crab cake mix should form a ball and hold its shape. If too dry, add more mayonnaise if needed; if too wet, add a little more breadcrumbs. Use 1-inch scoop to measure out crab cakes; form into flat discs about 1-inch round and ½-inch thick. In a sauté pan over medium-high heat, add just enough oil to coat bottom; place 6 to 8 crab cakes and fry on one side until golden, about 1 minute; turn over and fry until golden, about 1 minute. Drain on a paper towel and serve or keep warm in a 200-degree oven. The cakes may be pre-made and reheated in a 350-degree oven or frozen raw or cooked.

Chef's Note: For Tiburon Point Crab Cakes, use Dungeness or Rock Crab meat and omit the lemon zest and celery, also add just a bit more Old Bay seasoning.

WARM CREOLE RÉMOULADE

This sauce may be used on just about any seafood dish; use it like you would a tartar or cocktail sauce. It goes great with fish and chips and gives deep fried calamari a new twist. I also use it as a marinade for firm flesh fish that I am going to grill.

Yield: approximately ¾ cup sauce

Ingredients:

6 tablespoons Creole or whole grain mustard
2 tablespoons prepared Chile Sauce
2 tablespoons horseradish
1 tablespoon white wine
1 teaspoon olive oil
1 teaspoon chopped shallot
1 teaspoon chopped parsley
1 teaspoon Tabasco sauce

Directions: In a small saucepan, add ingredients and stir over medium-high heat until simmering; do not boil. If too thick, add a little more wine to reach desired thickness.

DIJON VINAIGRETTE

This is a classic French-style vinaigrette. The mustard helps to emulsify as well as add a little heat to the dressing. Don't be afraid to use this dressing as a marinade for chicken or rabbit or lamb. You may also change the type of mustard to a whole grain or flavored mustard.

Yield: 1 cup vinaigrette

Ingredients:
¼ cup red or white wine vinegar
1 tablespoon Dijon mustard
½ teaspoon sugar
1 medium shallot, finely minced
¾ cup olive oil
sea salt, to taste
freshly ground black pepper, to taste

Directions: In a mixing bowl or food-processing bowl, add vinegar and sugar; mix well. Add Dijon mustard and shallots, and whisk or process to begin to emulsify. Slowly add oil while whisking or processing a few drops at first, then in a very slow stream until the oil is fully emulsified. Add a pinch of salt and a few grinds of black pepper. Mix well and test with a piece of lettuce. If too tart for your taste, add a small amount of sugar.

TRIPLE CHOCOLATE TORTE

If you love chocolate, this cake will become your favorite. It is simple to make and a little slice goes a long way; it's quite rich.

Yield: one 9-inch killer cake, serves 12

Ingredients: Cake

1 cup unsalted butter, 2 sticks
8 ounces semi-sweet chocolate
1 cup unsweetened cocoa powder
1½ cups granulated sugar
6 large eggs
⅓ cup cognac
2 cups pecans finely chopped
cocoa powder for dusting
1 nine-inch spring form pan

Royal Chocolate Frosting

4 tablespoons unsalted butter
5 ounces dark or bittersweet chocolate
2 tablespoons whole milk
1 teaspoon vanilla extract
8 raspberries, garnish
8 pecan halves, garnish

Directions: Preheat oven to 350/F degrees, with rack in middle of oven. Line the bottom of a nine-inch spring form pan with wax paper; butter paper and sides; dust sides with cocoa powder. Melt butter and semi-sweet chocolate together in the top of a double boiler, or in a heatproof bowl set over simmering water. Set aside to cool. Sift the cocoa powder into a bowl. Add the eggs and stir until just combined. Add melted chocolate and cognac. Fold in ¾ of the chopped pecans, then pour batter into the prepared pan.

Bake until the cake is firm to the touch, about 45 minutes. Let the cake stand to cool for 15 minutes, then carefully unmold and transfer to a cooling rack, leaving cake on spring form bottom. Wrap cake in wax paper and refrigerate for at least 6 hours to overnight.

For the Royal Chocolate Frosting, combine the butter, dark chocolate, milk and vanilla in the top of a double boiler, or in a heatproof bowl set over simmering water until melted. Place a piece of wax paper under cake. Drizzle spoonfuls of the melted chocolate frosting along the edge; it should drip down and coat the sides of the cake. Pour the remaining frosting on the top of the cake, and with a large spatula even out the frosting. Reserve remaining frosting. As the frosting starts to set, cover the sides of the cake with the remaining pecans, gently pressing them on the sides with your hands. Transfer the cooling frosting to a piping bag with a large star tip. Make 12 small swirl mounds at each hand of the clock. Garnish swirl with a pecan half or raspberry.

Triple Chocolate Torte

APPLE WOOD SMOKED BACON
with DATES AND ALMONDS

You can never have too many of these tasty treats. I love the juxtaposition of the sweetness of the date, the saltiness of the bacon, and the crunchiness of the almond. The smoky flavor of the bacon just seems to meld all of the flavors together. I think this is my most popular appetizer.

Yield: 24 appetizers (not nearly enough)

Ingredients:

24 pitted dates, Medjool or any large date
24 whole raw almonds
12 slices apple wood smoked bacon, cut in half
24 toothpicks

Directions: Preheat oven to 350 degrees. Cut bacon in half. Place a whole almond inside of the date. Place a half slice of bacon on work board. Place the date on one end and roll while gently stretching the bacon to make it taut. Secure the loose end of bacon with a toothpick.

Appetizers may be refrigerated in an airtight container for up to two days. Place appetizers on a sheet pan or baking sheet with a lip. Bake in oven for 10 to 15 minutes or until bacon is crispy, not burnt. Remove from oven and drain on paper towel; serve hot, leaving toothpick as handle.

Chef's Note:

You can figure each person to eat at least 4 of these treats.

NEW RED POTATOES
with CHORIZO AND CUMIN CREAM

This appetizer has a Southwestern flair to it, but fits right in with just about any party. Make sure you use Mexican style chorizo. I prefer pork chorizo flavor over the beef chorizo, but both work just fine.

Yield: 24 appetizers

Ingredients:

12 new potatoes, red, gold or white
1 pound chorizo, fried to almost crispy
2 teaspoons ground cumin, lightly toasted
1 cup sour cream
salt, to taste
24 fresh cilantro leaves
melon baller

Directions: Cook chorizo in a sauté pan until all of the fat has been extracted, and chorizo looks dark and crumbly; drain and reserve meat. In a large pot, add washed potatoes and one tablespoon of salt. Bring potatoes to a boil and cook until just knife tender. Drain and cool potatoes. Cut cool potatoes in half; slightly trim round bottom, so they will sit flat; hollow out potatoes from half-cut side, leaving some potato flesh so potatoes hold their shape. Add some chorizo to potato; don't pack down, but slightly mound just above the rim of the potato. Potatoes may be refrigerated in an airtight container for up to two days.

In a sauté pan, add ground cumin and toast over medium-high heat, shaking pan so cumin won't burn. Remove from heat and cool. In a mixing bowl, add sour cream, a pinch of salt and some of the toasted cumin. Mix until creamy, adjusting salt and cumin to desired flavor;

place cumin cream in a squeeze bottle for easy distribution.

Preheat oven to 350 degrees. Put chorizo-filled potatoes on a baking sheet and place in oven. Bake for about 10 minutes to reheat. Remove from oven; squirt or spoon some cumin cream on top of chorizo; place a fresh cilantro sprig on top and serve warm.

Chef's Note:

You can also hollow out the rounded end of the potato and let it sit on the flat cut side, for a different presentation. Also, if you don't want to use chorizo, use your favorite brand of chile.

CROSTINI with SUN-DRIED TOMATO TAPÉNADE TOPPED with BRIE AND MANGO CHUTNEY

I am borrowing this recipe from my good friend, Chef Ian Morrison. Use the Crostini recipe (page 120) for the base of this appetizer. The sun-dried tomato tapénade also makes a wonderful pasta sauce or pizza sauce. Although the tapénade is easy to make, you may also use store bought to take a little stress off preparing for your party.

Yield: 24 appetizers

Ingredients:

24 crostini
1 cup sun-dried tomatoes
1 cup white wine
1 clove garlic, minced
1 shallot, minced
1 teaspoon dried oregano
1 bay leaf
½ teaspoon kosher salt
½ cup extra virgin olive oil
24 small slices of Brie
½ cup Major Grey's Mango Chutney

Directions: In a saucepot, add sun-dried tomatoes, white wine, minced garlic, minced shallot, bay leaf and salt. Bring to a boil and reduce heat to a simmer. Simmer until tomatoes are fully reconstituted and tender; add more wine or water if needed. Discard bay leaf and drain. Place the tomato mixture in a food processor and pulse. Add olive oil and pulse to blend; adjust salt. Allow mixture to cool. Tapénade may be kept in an airtight container for up to one week in the refrigerator or frozen up to 3 months.

With a butter knife or very small spatula, spread some of the tapénade mixture over the crostini. Place a small slice of Brie on top of tapénade. Place ½ teaspoon of chutney over Brie. Heat in oven until Brie just begins to melt. Serve warm.

Chef's Note:

So far I have found "Roland" brand to be the best chutney for color and flavor.

Sun-dried Tomato Tapénade Crostini
shown along with Bacon Wrapped Dates

AHI TUNA with WASABI CREAM AND GINGER CAVIAR IN A CUCUMBER TOWER

This is probably one of the best looking appetizers, not to mention one of my favorites. I love the Ahi tuna with the crispness of English cucumber. Of course, you may use other types of caviar, like wasabi or wasabe, flying fish roe, or any dark caviar. But, try to find gingered caviar, always use the best caviar you can find, and don't use or buy one that isn't chilled.

Yield: 24 appetizers

Ingredients:

3 English cucumbers
1 pound Ahi tuna, sushi grade
2 ounces ginger caviar, Tsar Nicoula Caviar
1 ounce wasabi paste
½ cup sour cream
1 teaspoon rice wine vinegar

Directions: Rinse the cucumbers. With a channeling knife, make one long groove down the length of the cucumber. Place your thumb in the groove and use it as a guide to make even distance grooves in the cucumber until fluted. Or, peel and make shallow grooves with a fork. Lay cucumber on cutting board and with a knife cut off the tip; move up the cucumber about ¾- to ⅞-inch thick and make a 90-degree cut. With a melon baller, make a shallow hole on cut side of cucumber about ¼-inch deep, making a shallow bowl (do not cut through cucumber bottom). They may be covered with a damp paper towel in an airtight container in the refrigerator for up to two days.

Cut Ahi tuna into ¼-inch cubes and keep in an

airtight container in the refrigerator for up to two days. Mix wasabi paste with teaspoon of rice wine vinegar into a smooth paste. Blend paste with sour cream. This may be kept in an airtight container in refrigerator for up to two days.

Place enough of the cubed Ahi in the hollowed out cucumber. Top with wasabi cream and some ginger caviar.

Chef's Note:

Use a crinkle cut knife for a nicer look on the cucumber. This can also be used with bay shrimp and cocktail sauce, a chicken salad with curry cream, or just whipped blue cheese, and you have several different appetizers.

NAWLIN'S STYLE SHRIMP
with TANGY COCKTAIL SAUCE

You can make this appetizer up to a day ahead and have the shrimp ready to serve. Use whatever size shrimp you like. I prefer the shrimp peeled with tails on, 16 to 18 per pound. You may also use the creole rémoulade in place of the cocktail sauce.

Yield: 8 servings of appetizers

Ingredients:

1½ pounds of 16-18 peeled shrimp with tails on, deveined
1 lemon, halved
2 tablespoons Old Bay seasoning or Shrimp Boil
1 teaspoon Tabasco sauce, or to taste
3 tablespoons Old Bay seasoning

Cocktail Sauce

12 ounces chile sauce
3 tablespoons horseradish
8 drops Tabasco sauce
2 tablespoons lemon juice
1 teaspoon parsley, chopped finely

Directions: In a large saucepot, fill up halfway with water; add lemon halves, Old Bay or Shrimp or Crab Boil and Tabasco. This step is called "a boil." Bring the boil to a boil; in batches, add shrimp and cook until shrimp just turns pink. Remove shrimp and drain, adding the next batch as needed. Place cooked and well-drained shrimp in a bowl; sprinkle with 3 tablespoons Old Bay seasoning and toss to coat well. Chill shrimp until served. This may be done up to 4 hours ahead.

Place seasoned shrimp either in a pile or in a circular shape on a tray with cocktail sauce in the middle.

Chef's Note:

For a real treat, add the spice coating to raw shrimp and sauté in butter (known as Cajun barbecue shrimp), then toss with cooked pasta, with a fresh squeeze of lemon juice.

Don't waste that boil; you can also boil corn on the cob, which will spice it up a whole lot, and new potatoes for a tangy salad.

TIGER PRAWNS AND SCALLOPS
ON BABY BOK CHOY

By increasing the amount of shrimp and scallops, this appetizer could easily become a main course.

Yield: 8 appetizers

Ingredients:

24 tiger prawns, 16-18 count
8 large sea scallops
4 baby bok choy, cut in half
1 tablespoon fresh ginger, minced
1 clove garlic, minced
1 tablespoon sesame oil
1 teaspoon peanut or vegetable oil
1 star of anise
1 tablespoon cornstarch
1 tablespoon lemon juice
2 tablespoons cold water
2 teaspoons soy sauce, low sodium

Directions: Peel and devein prawns, including tails. Remove the muscle from the sides of the scallops. Cut baby bok choy in half and rinse under cold water and drain. In a small bowl, add cornstarch and cold water. Stir until it becomes a slurry; add lemon juice and soy sauce.

In a large sauté pan or wok, over high heat, add peanut oil, sesame oil, star of anise, ginger, prawns and scallops. Sauté until prawns are pink and scallops translucent. Remove from pan. Add more oil if needed. Add bok choy halves and garlic; sauté until the white ends are just beginning to soften; add shrimp and scallops to bok choy; add cornstarch slurry and bring to a boil. Remove the star of anise and serve. Place a baby bok choy half on plate with cut side up; place three shrimp on fanned greens and a scallop on the stem; spoon over any remaining sauce and serve.

SPRING AND BITTER GREENS
with HOISIN VINAIGRETTE

This is a great Asian salad, which could be served at any barbecue or dinner. Add some grilled chicken to it, and you have a great lunch entrée.

Yield: 8 servings

Ingredients:

4 ounces baby salad greens
2 ounces baby arugula
½ cup pea sprouts
1 tablespoon hoisin sauce
1 tablespoon rice vinegar
1 teaspoon ginger juice
2 teaspoons sesame seed oil
8 pink grapefruit sections
2 star fruit, sliced
½ cup crispy chow mein noodles

Directions: Grate fresh ginger and squeeze, and reserve juice from pulp. Section grapefruit by cutting, both peeling and pith off the grapefruit with a paring knife. Cut off the stem end and bottom; sit grapefruit flat and make small cuts from top edge to bottom, removing about ½ inch of peel and pith with each cut, turning grapefruit after each cut; repeat until grapefruit is fully peeled. With knife blade, make a slicing cut along the membrane on one section of grapefruit, then cut the other side of section and cut away from center, exposing the grapefruit section. Repeat until you have 8 sections and reserve. Rinse and slice star fruit into about ⅛ inch thick slices and reserve.

In a medium-sized bowl, add hoisin sauce, rice vinegar and whisk until blended; add ginger, juice and whisk again. Whisk in sesame seed oil. Place some of the vinaigrette in a smaller bowl and reserve.

Place baby salad and arugula greens in the larger bowl and coat well. Place in center of salad plate. Toss pea sprouts in smaller bowl just to coat. Place pea sprouts on top of and in center of salad greens. Place one grapefruit section and star fruit slice on salad and sprinkle some crunchy chow mein noodles as garnish and serve.

TERIYAKI CHICKEN SKEWERS

These skewers may be cooked on the barbecue grill, on a stovetop grill, or even in the oven. The chicken may be marinated up to one day ahead of time. Serve this dish with white rice.

Yield: 8 servings

Ingredients:

24 long wooden skewers
8 chicken breasts, skinless and boneless
1 pineapple, cored, peeled and ¾-inch cubed
1 tablespoon fresh pineapple juice
1 cup teriyaki sauce
1 teaspoon ginger juice
1 clove garlic, finely minced
1 teaspoon sesame seeds

Directions: Slice chicken breasts into 3 or 4 equal slices and cut slices into cubes. Cut top and bottom off pineapple; cut peel away from pineapple. Slice pineapple into quarters lengthwise. Slice away core from center of each pineapple quarter. Cut cored quarters into ¾-inch cubes.

In a bowl, add teriyaki sauce, ginger juice and minced garlic and blend well. Add chicken cubes, cover, and chill for one hour. Place wooden skewers in water to soak.

Place a chicken cube on skewer; add a piece of pineapple, repeating as desired, leaving at least 2 inches of skewer as a handle on blunt end.

Preheat oven to 400 degrees. Spray sheet pan with spray oil; place chicken skewers on the sheet pan, and sprinkle with sesame seeds. Bake for 15 to 20 minutes until chicken is cooked. Serve 3 chicken skewers hot.

ASPARAGUS TIPS with WATER CHESTNUTS AND BLACK BEAN SAUCE

This vegetable dish is not only colorful, but also goes quite well with grilled salmon, or as a vegetarian main dish over plain rice.

Yield: 8 servings

Ingredients:

40 pencil size asparagus
1 small can sliced water chestnuts, rinsed and drained
1 teaspoon chopped garlic
1 teaspoon fresh ginger, peeled and minced
1 teaspoon sesame seed oil
1 teaspoon peanut or vegetable oil
½ cup Black Bean Sauce*
1 tablespoon cornstarch
1 green onion, sliced into bias slivers

Directions: Cut asparagus stems about ½ inch below the tips. Drain and rinse the water chestnuts. In a small bowl, add cornstarch and 2 tablespoons of cold water; mix until well blended and add black bean sauce.

In a hot, but not smoking wok or sauté pan, add peanut and sesame oil. To hot oil, add chopped garlic, ginger and asparagus tips and sliced water chestnuts. Stir-fry or sauté until tips just begin to change in color to a bright green. Add black bean mixture and allow sauce to come to a boil to thicken (the sauce should become shiny). Add sliced green onions and serve.

Chef's Note:

Since asparagus can be costly in many parts of the states, you may use the stems of the asparagus, cutting them on a bias about one-inch long. Peel any stems that are bigger than a pencil. If serving vegetables family-style, place sliced green onion on top of the asparagus as a garnish.

*Black Bean Sauce may be found in the Asian food section of your supermarket.

SNICKERDOODLE COOKIES

These cookies are very easy to make, and are perfect for the beginning baker to try. I have served them with hot chocolate and even green tea ice cream.

Yield: 20-40 cookies

Ingredients:
1 cup margarine, room temperature
1-⅓ cup sugar
2 large eggs
3 cups all-purpose flour
1½ teaspoons cream of tartar
1 teaspoon baking soda
1 pinch salt
1 tablespoon milk

Cinnamon Coating
2 tablespoons sugar
1½ teaspoons ground cinnamon
½ teaspoon ground star anise (for Asian cookies only)
¼ cup pine nuts, garnish

Directions: Preheat oven to 375 degrees. Prepare cinnamon coating. In large bowl, mix margarine, sugar and eggs until fluffy; add milk and dry ingredients and blend well. Roll dough into 1" balls. Roll balls in cinnamon sugar coating. Place balls 2½ inches apart on an ungreased cookie sheet with parchment. Flatten balls slightly and place one pine nut on top of each. Bake for 10 minutes or until golden; remove and cool on rack.

Chef's Note:

You can use up to 2 tablespoons ground pine nuts, or replace the pine nuts with another type. You can even add chocolate chips.

GARLIC BUTTERED CORN ON THE COB

I know, you're thinking, "Who doesn't know how to butter corn on the cob?" Well, try this recipe to really wow your family and friends. Don't be afraid to buy frozen corn on the cob during the off season, since it's picked fresh and frozen within hours after picking.

Yield: 8 servings

Ingredients:
8 fresh corn on the cob, white or yellow
1 cube unsalted butter
1 tablespoon Jack Daniel's Whiskey
1 medium shallot, finely minced
3 cloves garlic, finely minced
1 teaspoon parsley, chopped finely
¼ teaspoon freshly ground black pepper
½ teaspoon sea or kosher salt
4 dashes Tabasco sauce
salt for water
4 cloves garlic for water

Directions: In a medium saucepot, add everything but the corn. Bring to a very low simmer and allow butter to slowly cook the garlic and shallot over low heat, about 20 minutes. If butter begins to brown, remove from heat. Remove garlic butter from heat and reserve. At this point, you may use it melted or allow it to cool until you can spoon it onto wax or parchment paper. Roll the butter up tight, forming a cylinder and chill. Once hardened, cut butter into rounds for use. Or, my favorite is to put the semi-soft butter into a piping bag that's fitted with a fluted star tip, then pipe out little butter kisses on a cookie sheet. Chill until used.
Bring a large pot with salted water to a heavy boil.

Shuck corn, removing leaves and silk. Place corn in pot and cook about 3 to 5 minutes, or until tender.

Chef's Note:

If you wish, you may add other flavorings to the water, such as cayenne, lemons or fresh dill, all of which will add flavor to the corn.

SLAP YOURSELF CORN BREAD

This corn bread is so good that you'll have to slap yourself to believe it. I always make a double batch, just so I have some to snack on. It also makes a great filler for stuffings, not to mention for breakfast, toasted with honey, butter, a good cup of coffee, and a cowboy movie on the television.

Yield: 9 servings

Ingredients:
2 tablespoons unsalted butter, melted
2 cups yellow stone-ground corn meal
1 cup all-purpose flour
2 teaspoons baking powder
½ teaspoon baking soda
4 teaspoons sugar
2 large eggs
⅔ cup buttermilk
⅔ cup whole milk
butter for greasing baking pan

Directions: Preheat oven to 425 degrees. Place oven rack in the center position. Grease a 9-inch square baking pan with butter. In a large bowl, whisk the dry ingredients together; make a well in the dry ingredients. Crack the eggs in a separate bowl (to prevent shells) and add to well, stirring lightly with a wooden spoon to just break yolks and mix with whites; add buttermilk and milk. Quickly stir ingredients until almost combined; add melted butter and stir until just combined (do not overwork the batter). Pour batter into baking pan and place in oven. Bake until corn bread is lightly browned, and the edges have slightly pulled away from sides; the top may be lightly cracked. Transfer to a cooling rack and cool corn bread for about 8 minutes. Cut corn bread into desired size slices and serve warm.

Chef's Note:

I love to serve the corn bread with either maple butter or honey butter. Take a stick of room temperature, unsalted butter and cut into pieces. Place pieces in food processor and process until soft; add 2 tablespoons of honey or maple syrup and blend. Place flavored butter in a shallow bowl to serve. You can use what I do at home—a good old-fashioned cast-iron pan—to make the corn bread.

MAPLE BAKED BEANS

There are times that I cheat a little, and this is one of them. When I am making baked beans in quantity, I always use "Bushes Baked Beans," and as we say in the industry, "Fix-um-up."

Yield: serves a crowd

Ingredients:

1 gallon #10 can Bushes Baked Beans
2 cups maple syrup
1 cup molasses
½ cup Jack Daniel's Whiskey
2 tablespoons dry mustard
2 tablespoons Lea & Perrins Worcestershire Sauce
½ cup white onions, chopped finely
1 tablespoon garlic, minced finely
½ teaspoon black pepper

Directions: Preheat oven to 350 degrees. Open the can and pour beans into a large ovenproof container. In a mixing bowl, add remaining ingredients and blend until mustard is fully incorporated. Add maple mix to the beans and gently stir. Cover beans with lid or foil and place in oven for about 30 minutes or until beans are bubbling.

LEMON ACHIOTE MARINADE

Achiote is the product of the annatto seed, which is ground into a paste. It has a brick-red to orange color, and may be found in the Mexican food section of most stores. This paste is mixed with different spices, which gives both color and flavor to meats, sauces, rice or masa when used. Annatto is what gives butter its yellow coloring. We will use the Achiote as a base for our marinade. This base can go in several different directions, such as using citrus juices, liquors, flavored or infused oils, and additional spices. This marinade works well with seafood and poultry. I have also used it on game meats and fowl.

Yield: 8 servings

Ingredients:

8 half chicken breasts, skin on, bone in
2 tablespoons achiote paste
1 clove garlic, minced
1 tablespoon rosemary
1 teaspoon ground cumin
1 teaspoon ground coriander
1 teaspoon salt
1 cup lemon juice
¼ cup olive oil

Directions: Rinse and pat dry chicken. In a mixing bowl, break up achiote; add the remaining ingredients and mix well. Add chicken breasts and coat well on all sides; move skin with fingers and rub marinade under skin (this may be done up to a day ahead).

Preheat oven to 400 degrees. Remove excess marinade from chicken. Do not rinse. Place marinated chicken breasts on baking sheet and bake in oven for 20 to

35 minutes or until juices are clear, and a thermometer gives an internal reading of 160 degrees. Remove from oven and let rest for five minutes. The chicken may also be grilled or barbecued.

Chef's Note:
Try adding tequila to the marinade for a kick.

MARGARITA SAUCE

This sauce goes well with the Lemon Achiote Chicken, achiote-crusted pork tenderloin or barbecued chicken.

Yield: 1 cup sauce

Ingredients:

1 cup tequila
½ cup triple sec or ½ cup orange juice
1 cup lime juice
1 teaspoon kosher salt
1 cube unsalted butter, 4 ounces

Directions: In a heavy saucepan, add tequila, triple sec or orange juice, and lime juice. Place over medium-high heat and allow to simmer (it may flame up, just allow it to burn itself out). Simmer until reduced to ¼ cup of liquid. Remove from heat and add the cube of cold butter and stir until fully melted and emulsified. Keep warm and serve warm.

Chef's Note:

If you don't want to use alcohol in the sauce, replace it with margarita mix.

CHEF CLYDE'S
TEXAS DRY RUBBED TRI-TIP

This dry rub works well on all meats, especially on pork ribs.

Yield: 8 servings

Ingredients:
2 tri-tip steaks
1 tablespoon kosher or sea salt
1 tablespoon ancho chile
1 tablespoon chile powder
1 tablespoon hot paprika
1 teaspoon dried oregano, hand crushed
1 teaspoon lemon zest, minced
1 teaspoon black pepper
1 teaspoon granulated garlic
1 teaspoon onion powder
1 teaspoon dried thyme, hand crushed

Directions: Mix all dry ingredients in a mixing bowl. Trim tri-steaks of any silver skin and excess fat. Take a handful of dry rub and spread it on the meat, rubbing it in. This may be done up to 4 hours ahead of cooking.

Preheat oven to 475 degrees. Spray a light coat of oil on tri-tips and place tri-tips on a sheet pan on middle rack of oven; reduce heat to 450 degrees. Roast for 10 to 12 minutes for rare (internal temperature of 125 degrees), 18 to 20 minutes for medium-rare (internal temperature of 140 degrees). Check temperatures in the thickest part of tri-tip. Remove beef from oven and allow meat to rest for at least 5 minutes before carving. Tri-tips may also be grilled or barbecued, following the same internal temperatures for doneness.

Chef's Note:

If the ancho chile powder is not available, use a bit more chile powder.

CHIPOTLE BARBECUE SAUCE

This smoky, slightly hot sauce not only makes a great barbecue sauce for beef, chicken or pork, but also makes a fantastic sauce for pulled meat sandwiches or "Sloppy Joes."

Yield: 2 to 3 cups of sauce

Ingredients:

3 cups tomato sauce
½ cup tomato paste
½ cup brown sugar, packed
½ cup apple cider vinegar
¼ cup white wine
2 tablespoons puréed chipotle en adobo, or to taste
2 tablespoons Worcestershire Sauce
1 tablespoon molasses
1 teaspoon kosher salt
1 teaspoon garlic, finely minced
½ teaspoon dried oregano, hand crushed

Directions: Purée the chipotle chiles with their sauce in a food processor. In large saucepot, add all of the ingredients. Blend well and simmer over medium heat 20 minutes; taste for heat of chipotle and sweetness; adjust as needed. Continue to simmer until reduced to 2 to 3 cups. Serve warm. Sauce may be kept in an airtight container in refrigerator for up to two weeks.

Chef's Note:

This barbecue sauce tastes better after a few days. If it's too thick, it can be thinned with water, tequila or fruit juices to give it a kick.

Chipotle chiles are dried and smoked jalapeño chiles. The chiles are then rehydrated in an adobo sauce. They have some heat to them and a wonderful smoky flavor and scent.

PASSOVER MATZO BALLS (*KNAIDELS*)

Use this recipe for Chicken Soup with Knaidels (matzo balls) and Carrot Pearls (next recipe). They are also used like dumplings to top the Tsimmes recipe.

Yield: 14 to 20 matzo balls

Ingredients:
4 large whole eggs
4 tablespoons chicken soup (page 165)
1 teaspoon kosher salt
⅛ teaspoon white pepper
4 tablespoons rendered chicken fat (*schmaltz*)
1 cup matzo meal
chicken stock or water

Directions: Beat eggs well. Add chicken soup, rendered chicken fat, salt and pepper; mix well. Add matzo meal and mix until uniformly moist and mixed. Do not over mix.

Let stand covered in refrigerator for 1 hour or longer. Chill hands with ice water and place a tablespoon of mixture into hand and form a round ball. Bring a large pot of salted water or chicken stock to a rolling boil. Place balls in boiling salted water and cover; allow water to return to a low boil and boil for 45 minutes to 1 hour. Remove from liquid and allow to cool.

Chef's Note:
The cooked matzo balls may be done a day or two ahead and kept refrigerated in an airtight container. They are used as garnish in the Chicken Soup and in the Tsimmes.

CHICKEN SOUP
with KNAIDELS AND CARROT PEARLS

Everyone loves chicken soup. This is the simplest way to make it no fuss, and it's fast. You can use the soup as a stock or incorporate other vegetables, pasta, even rice, to change it up a little.

Yield: 8 cups soup

Ingredients:

1 whole chicken, rinsed
2 celery ribs, halved
½ onion, quartered
½ carrot, peeled and cut into thick rounds
2 parsley sprigs
salt, to taste
3 large carrots, peeled
matzo balls (Knaidels)

Directions: In a stockpot, fill with enough cold water to cover a whole chicken, about 2 quarts. Remove fat (save for matzo balls) and chicken heart, gizzard and liver from the cavity of the chicken. Rinse well.

Place chicken in pot of cold water and add vegetables. Bring to a boil and reduce to a simmer, skimming any fat and scum from the top. Let chicken simmer until flesh pulls away from the ends of the legs. Remove soup from heat. Remove chicken from soup or stock. Let chicken cool enough to touch. Discard skin and pull chicken off the bones and reserve separated bones and meat. Taste stock; if it has enough flavor, strain and cool. If it tastes watery, add chicken bones and bring it back to a simmer for about 30 minutes. Drain soup and cool, discarding all solids and reserving the broth.

Peel 3 large carrots; cut into 3- or 4-inch long sections. Place carrots in cold water and bring to a boil in lightly salted water. Test with a knife; when it goes in with just some resistance, carrots are done. Drain and rinse under cold water. When carrots are cooled, use a small ⅛-inch Parisian scoop or tiny melon baler, to scoop out pearls from the cooked carrots. Reserve pearls.

Heat soup to a little above serving temperature; add matzo balls. Add shredded chicken, carrot pearls and a couple of matzo balls to soup bowl; fill with broth and serve.

Chef's Note:

If you are going to serve noodles or rice with the soup, cook separately and rinse under running water and drain before adding to the soup, or it will cloud the broth. Also, if the broth is still a little watery, just let it reduce a little longer to enrichen the flavor.

SALAD OF TENDER FIELD GREENS
with TOASTED WALNUTS
AND A SHALLOT VINAIGRETTE

I love field greens; the baby greens have some bitterness and sweetness to them, making a host for a flavorful vinaigrette. You could replace or make a combination of the field greens with butter lettuce or baby spinach.

Yield: 12 servings

Ingredients:

6 ounces baby field greens, rinsed and dried
4 ounces walnut halves, toasted
4 ounces freshly shaved Parmesan cheese

Shallot Vinaigrette:

3 tablespoons shallot vinegar "Arnabal Intl."
  or 3 tablespoons champagne vinegar
1 teaspoon chopped shallots
1 teaspoon sugar
sea or kosher salt, to taste
freshly ground black pepper, to taste
¼ cup olive oil

Directions: In a small mixing bowl, add shallot vinegar, chopped shallots, salt and freshly ground black pepper. Whisk until sugar and salt have dissolved. Slowly add olive oil while whisking to fully emulsify. Chill vinaigrette until needed.

In a sauté pan, over high heat, add walnut halves; stir and toast until edges become dark brown, but not burnt. Remove from heat and let cool.

In a large mixing bowl, add some shallot vinaigrette. Add baby field greens, toss to coat well, adding more dressing if needed. Place some of the dressed salad in the center of each plate; with a vegetable peeler, shave the Parmesan cheese over salad, and add a few toasted walnut halves and serve.

OVEN ROASTED ASPARAGUS
with PUMPKIN SEED OIL

Oven roasting is my favorite way of cooking asparagus. When you steam or boil the asparagus, color, flavor and nutrients are left behind—just look at the water. Not only that, but you can also cook a load of them at once. Personally, I like the thicker asparagus, when peeled, over the pencil asparagus. This method works for green, white or purple asparagus. The addition of the pumpkin seed oil with its dark green color and roasted nutty flavor not only adds dimension of color and flavor to the dish, but also a whole lot of omega 3s to it.

Yield: 12 servings

Ingredients:

60 asparagus stalks
1 teaspoon olive oil
sea salt or kosher salt
1 tablespoon Pumpkin Seed Oil

Directions: Preheat oven to 400 degrees. If asparagus is thicker than a pencil, gently peel with vegetable peeler. Place tips so they are in a straight line and cut the bottoms off evenly, so all asparagus are the same size. On a cookie sheet with sides, place the asparagus with tips all facing the same side. Add the olive oil, salt and black pepper. Toss gently to coat.

Place asparagus in preheated oven and let roast for 10 to 12 minutes. Take one out of the middle to test. If done, remove from oven and keep warm, but not hot, or they will overcook and discolor. Place on plate or in chafing dish (if using a chafing dish, use low or no heat once bottom water is hot); place with tips to the same side. And drizzle pumpkin seed oil over the tips and stems.

TSIMMES
with CHICKEN AND BEEF

Use this rich stew as your entrée for Passover. It has a unique sweet and sour flavor. By dredging the meat in matzo flour, it acts as both a thickener and adds flavor to the dish. Serve along with chicken soup with matzo balls and gefilte fish.

Yield: 30 servings as entrée or side dish

Ingredients:
4 pounds chicken, cut into pieces
½ pound dried prunes, pitted
4 pounds beef brisket or shoulder meat, cubed
½ pound dried apricots, halved
3 cups carrots, sliced into rounds
½ cup golden raisins
3 cups sweet potatoes, sliced ½-inch thick
½ cup dark raisins
3 cups baking potato, quartered, sliced ½-inch thick
3 stalks celery, peeled and sliced
½ cup dark brown sugar
3 to 4 lemons, sliced thinly
kosher salt, to taste
freshly ground black pepper, to taste
water to cover
potato starch or matzo ball flour
olive oil
1 Matzo Ball Recipe (Knaidels)

Directions: Dredge cubed beef in potato flour. In heavy stewpot, add olive oil and brown beef; add chicken. Place matzo balls on top of meat and cover with carrots, potatoes and celery; add dried fruit and lemon slices. Cover with cold water by 1 inch and add salt, pepper and brown sugar. Bring to a boil; cover and reduce heat to a simmer for 1 hour. Check liquid and adjust seasoning with brown sugar and lemon juice. Place in a preheated oven for 3 hours.

To thicken stew, mix potato starch with cooking liquid; stir until smooth and add to tsimmes; place in oven until thickened.

Chef's Note:

Save the chicken fat or *schmaltz* for your matzo balls. This dish can be made a day or two ahead and just slowly reheated to serve.

CHOCOLATE TOFFEE CRISPS

This is a very simple dessert using matzo crackers.

Yield: 30 servings

Ingredients:

1 box matzo, about 15 crackers
1 cup margarine
1 cup brown sugar
8 ounces semi-sweet chocolate morsels
spray oil

Directions: Preheat oven to 300 degrees Fahrenheit. Line two or more cookie sheets with foil and lightly spray oil to coat. Break matzo in half and arrange over cookie sheet; it's okay to overlap if needed. In a small pan, melt margarine and brown sugar over low heat, stirring constantly until it bubbles. Pour over matzos and quickly but gently spread; it may not cover but that's okay. Sprinkle morsels over melted sugar mixture.

Place sheet pans in oven and bake for 5 minutes, or until chocolate has melted (some of the morsels may not look melted). If not spreadable, replace in oven for a few minutes more until chocolate can be easily spread. Spread melted chocolate quickly and evenly over matzos. Put trays in freezer until hardened, about 2 hours. Either use a pizza cutter or knife to score and break into squares or shapes or just break into bite-size pieces.

STRAWBERRY
RHUBARB CRUMBLE

As a rule, I don't care much for rhubarb. I mean, I don't like it at all. But, this dish wasn't that bad; I actually like it, which is a real stretch for me. Here you use the matzo crackers, as you would oatmeal on an apple crisp. Oh yeah, don't forget the sorbet.

Yield: 1 2-quart casserole

Ingredients:

Filling:

4 cups fresh rhubarb, rinsed, coarse-chopped, ½-inch pieces
1¾ cups sugar
1 cup water
2 large baskets of strawberries, rinsed and hulled
¼ cup quick cooking tapioca powder
½ teaspoon ground cinnamon
2 tablespoons lemon juice
1 pinch of kosher salt

Topping:

1 cup matzo crackers, ground
½ cup margarine
⅛ teaspoon ground nutmeg
1 pinch kosher salt
1 tablespoon sugar
spray oil

Directions: Preheat oven to 350 degrees/Fahrenheit. Spray a light coating of oil in a 2-quart, ovenproof casserole. In a non-corrosive pot, add the 4 cups of rhubarb, sugar and water. Bring to a boil, stirring until sugar is melted and rhubarb is tender, and the mixture has thickened slightly.

Allow to cool slightly. Add rhubarb to casserole dish. Add the hulled strawberries, tapioca powder, cinnamon and a pinch of salt. Blend well; taste for sweetness. If it seems too sweet, add a little lemon juice; if too tart, omit the juice and add a little more sugar.

Process, grind or crush the matzo crackers into a fine crumb. Add margarine, nutmeg and a pinch of salt and sugar to the matzo mix and blend well. Squeeze into compact lumps, then crumble over strawberry-rhubarb mixture. Bake for 35 to 40 minutes or until the top is golden brown and the strawberry mixture is bubbling hot. Allow to cool, but serve warm.

Chef's Note:

Chopped nuts may be added to the crumb mixture. Also, the berries may be replaced with raspberries, blackberries or boysenberries. Blueberries and even seedless grapes may be substituted or added for a change.

ASIAN SHRIMP PATTIES
with THAI GREEN CURRY

These patties use the small dried shrimp, which are used throughout Asia. The patties can be flavored with any type of Asian ingredient, as long as it does not overpower the shrimp flavor.

Yield: about 24 patties

Ingredients:
1 Thai Green Curry Sauce Recipe (page 177)
6 large eggs, separated
2 ounces small dried shrimp, ground finely
1 tablespoon fresh ginger, chopped finely
1 teaspoon finely chopped fresh garlic
1 tablespoon ginger juice
1 tablespoon freshly chopped cilantro
pinch cream of tartar
oil for frying

Directions: Grind dried shrimp into a fine powder in food processor. Separate eggs; beat the yolks until they change color, to a pale yellow; add ground shrimp, chopped ginger, chopped garlic, ginger juice and chopped cilantro. In a heavy frying pan, heat about ¼ inch of oil over medium heat. While oil is heating, add cream of tartar to egg whites and whip to a stiff peak. Mix ⅓ of whites into shrimp-yolk mixture; blend well to lighten yolk mixture. Gently fold in remaining whites into lightened yolk mixture. Spoon one dessertspoonful of mixture into hot oil (about silver-dollar size) and fry to a light golden color; turn over and fry to an even golden color. Drain on paper towel.

Place Asian Shrimp Patties in frying pan or heatable

serving platter and cover with Thai Green Curry Sauce (the sauce should be loose to allow the patties to soak up the sauce); heat and let simmer for five minutes and serve.

THAI GREEN CURRY SAUCE

Yield: makes 24 to 30 patties

Ingredients:

2 tablespoons Thai green curry paste, or to taste
2 cans coconut milk
2 tablespoons saki, optional
1 tablespoon finely chopped galanga or ginger
1 teaspoon chopped garlic
3 lemon grass stalks, white, chopped finely
2 tablespoons chopped cilantro leaf
1 teaspoon fish sauce

Directions: In a heavy saucepot over medium-high heat, stir in all of the coconut milk, saki, chopped galanga or ginger, chopped garlic, chopped lemon grass, chopped cilantro and fish sauce. Bring to a simmer; continue stirring for about 5 minutes. If sauce is too thick, thin with either water or saki to a desired consistency of half & half or a little thinner. Strain the sauce and serve.

Asian Shrimp Patties with Thai Green Curry Sauce

BLUE CRAB SALAD with CREOLE DRESSING ON BABY GREENS

This salad makes a wonderful starter or entrée salad. If you like bay shrimp, they may be added to the crab mix, which gives a little color and additional flavor to the salad. You may even want to try it with avocado slices, cucumber or tomato slices to the finished salad as a garnish.

Yield: 8 to 10 servings

Ingredients:

Crab Mix
1 pound blue crab lump meat
½ cup mayonnaise
1 tablespoon creole or whole grain mustard
½ cup celery, peeled and diced finely
1 teaspoon lemon juice
½ teaspoon freshly chopped dill
½ teaspoon finely chopped shallot
½ to 1 teaspoon Old Bay seasoning

Salad Dressing
¼ cup red wine vinegar or sherry vinegar
½ teaspoon chopped thyme
½ teaspoon finely chopped shallot
1 tablespoon creole mustard
1 teaspoon sugar, or to taste
kosher or sea salt to taste
freshly ground black pepper
½ cup olive oil
baby field greens or butter lettuce

Directions: In a medium-sized mixing bowl, add blue crab and all ingredients except for the salad greens. Mix well, but try not to break apart the lumps of crabmeat too much. Keep chilled until use. Depending on the moisture of the crabmeat, you may have to add some mayonnaise.

In a medium-sized mixing bowl, add dressing ingredients, except for oil; whisk to incorporate. Slowly add oil while whisking to emulsify. Adjust sugar, salt and pepper to taste. Keep chilled until use. Place washed baby greens in a medium-sized bowl; add some Creole Dressing and toss to coat. Place dressed greens on a plate and place a scoop of crab salad on top.

CALAMARI and PENNE PASTA
with SAFFRON CREAM SAUCE

Calamari is more commonly known as squid. Most of our calamari comes from Monterey, which is just south of San Francisco. If you love seafood, this dish can be made with prawns, a firm-fleshed fish such as swordfish, or snapper, but the purple, red and white of the cooked calamari show off the very expensive saffron.

Yield: serves 4

Ingredients:
1 pound penne pasta, or any pasta
½ pound whole calamari, frozen is okay
1 clove garlic, minced finely
1 shallot, minced finely
1 tablespoon olive oil
1 pint heavy cream
1 pinch Spanish or Greek saffron
1 tablespoon chopped parsley
¼ cup white wine

Directions: To clean calamari: cut mouth off and discard (it's in the center of the tentacles); cut tentacles from head, and head from body. Remove guts and clear quill from body; remove fins and discard. Rinse body and tentacles. Cut the body into ½-inch rings; leave tentacles whole.

Cook pasta in boiling salted water until al dente (slightly chewy); rinse under hot water and reserve. In a sauté pan, over medium-high heat, add olive oil. Sauté shallots, garlic and saffron; when shallots are translucent, add white wine and heavy cream; bring to a boil and reduce to a fairly thick sauce that will coat the back of a spoon. Add calamari and simmer for two minutes or until the rings have folded back and the tentacles have curled and changed color. Remove from heat; add pasta and toss to coat. Sprinkle with chopped parsley and serve.

Chef's Note:
Do not overcook the calamari, or it will become chewy.

CRUSTED PORK TENDERLOIN
AND VARIOUS DRY RUBS

Yield: serves 4 to 8

Ingredients:

1 or 2 pork tenderloins
sea or kosher salt
freshly ground black pepper
Dry Rub Spice (page 183)
2 tablespoons oil

Directions: Rinse meat and pat dry. Remove silver skin from tenderloins. Salt and pepper meat. Pat or rub spice on to tenderloins. In hot sauté pan or grill, add oil and tenderloin; gently turn until all sides are slightly brown. Place tenderloin in 350-400/F degree oven until tenderloin reaches an internal temperature of 132 degrees/F. Remove and let rest for 3 minutes before slicing.

CHEF CLYDE'S DRY RUBS

Directions: Grind spices; finely chop fresh herbs; add sea or kosher salt to taste, and blend with a small amount of oil. Pat the dry rub on meat and let rest, refrigerating for one hour to overnight. Grill and eat.

HERB
dried oregano
fresh parsley
fresh cilantro
fresh rosemary

NUT
pecan (optional)
walnut (optional
hazelnut (optional)
Dijon mustard
honey

MEDITERRANEAN
orange zest
lemon zest
oregano

LOVE RUB
(equal parts)
fine sugar
dried thyme
ground black pepper
kosher salt

ASIAN
star anise
coriander seed
cinnamon
sesame seed

SOUTHWESTERN
chile powder
garlic
ground cumin
chile powder

BLACK PEPPER
black pepper, cracked
fresh garlic

COFFEE
espresso, finely ground
black pepper, ground

SAN FRANCISCO CIOPPINO
San Francisco Shellfish Stew

Cioppino (cha-pen-o) is a classical shellfish stew, which is served all along the famous San Francisco Fisherman's Wharf. This hearty stew brings the best of the fisherman's catch to the table in a rich tomato broth. Hands are definitely permitted, along with a pair of nutcrackers to get that last bit of sweet crab. All that is needed with this dish is some nice crusty San Francisco sourdough bread and a nice glass of wine.

Yield: 4-6 servings

Ingredients:
1 tablespoon olive oil
¼ cup minced leek, white part only
¼ cup finely diced white onion
½ cup finely diced celery
½ cup finely diced carrot
3 whole green onions, chopped
1 tablespoon minced garlic
1 teaspoon crushed dried thyme
1 teaspoon dried oregano
1 teaspoon dried basil
1 teaspoon kosher salt
½ teaspoon black pepper, to taste
¼ teaspoon dry red pepper chile flakes (optional)
4 each Roma or plum tomatoes, peeled, seeded and diced
   or one 20-ounce can stewed tomatoes, chopped
1½ cups clam juice
1 cup dry white wine, Sauvignon blanc or dry vermouth
2 tablespoons lemon juice
2 pounds Dungeness cooked cracked crab
¾ pound shrimp, 26-32 count

¾ pound clams in shells
1 pound red snapper or swordfish (cut into ½-inch dice)
¼ cup fresh Italian parsley (chopped)

Directions: Place a large stewpot over medium heat; add olive oil, leeks, celery, carrot and onions; sauté until wilted. Add garlic, tomatoes with juice, clam juice and the wine. Bring to a simmer; add dry herbs and cooked cracked crab, shrimp and swordfish. Let simmer for 10 minutes; add clams, green onions, and chopped parsley and simmer until clam shells open (discard any which do not open), about five minutes; adjust seasoning.

DUNGENESS CRAB
with GINGER AND GARLIC

This dish is a combination of Chinese and Native American. The Native Americans learned to catch Dungeness crabs off the Pacific Coast in willow baskets and reed boats. It's the crab's sweet flavor that balances with the heat or the ginger and chiles.

Yield: 4 servings

Ingredients:

2 fresh Dungeness crabs, cleaned and cracked
1 tablespoon fresh ginger, minced
1 fresh Thai or Serrano chile, minced
4 cloves fresh garlic, minced
1 teaspoon flat leaf parsley, minced
1 green onion, cut into 4 pieces
1-2 tablespoons peanut oil

Directions: In a hot wok or sauté pan, add peanut oil and fresh crab. Stir-fry until color of crab changes; add ginger and minced chile, and stir. Continue to stir until crab is a bright orange-red color; add garlic, continuing to stir; add green onion and flat leaf parsley. Serve hot.

Chef's Note:

This dish may be made with any type of in-shell crab, crayfish, lobster or shrimp.

PANKO CRUSTED SALMON
with MANGO PAPAYA SALSA

The salmon may be substituted with any firm-flesh fish. The flavoring of the panko crust can also be changed to suit your needs.

Yield: 4 servings

Ingredients:

4 each 5- to 6-ounce Pacific salmon fillets, skin off and pin bones removed
1½ cups Panko breadcrumbs
2 tablespoons vegetable or light olive oil
1 teaspoon chopped parsley
1 teaspoon chopped thyme
1 teaspoon chopped dill
1 teaspoon paprika
sea or kosher salt, to taste
black pepper, to taste
vegetable oil, for sautéing

MANGO SALSA:

2 ripe mangos, peeled and diced small
1 ripe papaya, peeled, seeded and diced small
1 jalapeño chile, seeded and chopped finely
1 ounce rum (optional)
sea or kosher salt, to taste   1 Tsp. Chopped cilantro
black pepper, to taste

Directions: Cut top and bottom from mangos and papaya, then peel. Cut mango ⅛-inch off center and follow seed. Cut into ¼-inch dice and reserve in a bowl. Cut papaya in half, and remove and discard seeds. Cut into ¼-inch dice and reserve with mango. Cut tip from stem of chile and cut down sides leaving the veins and seeds intact. Dice chile into ⅛ inch dice and add to mango papaya mixture. Add rum and blend well, trying not to crush. Add chopped Cilantro

In a bowl, add panko, chopped parsley, ~~cilantro~~ Thyme and dill. Add one tablespoon of oil and blend well, adding more if needed. Panko mixture should be well oiled but not wet. Preheat oven to 400/F.

Season both sides of fish fillets with salt, pepper and paprika. Place fish skin side down; pat on panko mixture evenly on top of fillet, about ⅛-inch thick.

In a large hot ovenproof sauté pan (preferably non-stick), add one teaspoon oil and place crust side down and sauté until you can see the crust beginning to turn golden, about 3 minutes. Turn fillet over and continue to sauté for 1 minute, then place in oven for about 5 to 7 minutes until fish feels just firm when touched and crust is golden but not dark. Place two tablespoons on plate and place fillet on top of salsa.

PAN-SEARED SEA SCALLOPS IN PEPPER VODKA SAUCE

Yield: 8 servings

Ingredients:

36 to 40 diver sea scallops (round as a 50-cent piece)
vegetable oil (not olive oil)
ground paprika
lemon zest (chopped finely)
freshly ground black pepper
sea or kosher salt, to taste

Directions: In a bowl, add paprika, chopped lemon zest, black pepper and salt. Remove small mussel from sides of scallops. Place scallop in herb bowl with end down and press gently; turn over and press so both ends are coated. In a hot sauté pan, add oil; when oil is hot, but not smoking, place scallops with crusted-end side down; reduce heat slightly when sides of scallops change color almost halfway up; turn over and finish cooking. Remove and drain on paper towel.

Pepper Vodka Sauce:

2 tablespoons whole black peppercorns
4 ounces vodka (pepper or lemon vodka works great)
1 tablespoon chopped shallots
sea or kosher salt
4 ounces cold unsalted butter (in pieces)

Directions: In a dry hot sauté pan, add black pepper and toast, but do not burn. Add vodka and let come to a boil (careful—it will flame). When flames subside, add shallots and reduce heat; cook until translucent. Remove pan from heat; add a few pieces of butter and whisk until almost melted; add a few more pieces until desired consistency is reached. Keep warm but no over, direct heat or sauce will break.

CREAMED SPINACH

This is a classic side dish that is at home with prime rib or your Thanksgiving turkey. It can also be made with Swiss chard, collard greens or beet tops.

Yield: 10 servings

Ingredients:
3 pounds baby spinach
1¼ cup whole milk
1 cup heavy cream
2 shallots, finely chopped
1 clove garlic, pressed
¼ cup unsalted butter
¼ cup all-purpose flour
freshly grated nutmeg, to taste
sea or kosher salt, to taste
freshly ground black pepper, to taste
salt for water

Directions: Clean and rinse spinach. Place spinach in a pot with 1 inch of lightly salted boiling water. Stir constantly and cook for 1 to 2 minutes; cook in batches if needed. Drain spinach and rinse under cold running water until cool. Squeeze as much of the water out of the spinach as you can. Chop spinach coarsely; set aside.

Heat milk, heavy cream and garlic in a small saucepan over medium heat, stirring until warm. In a heavy 3-quart or medium-sized saucepan over medium-low heat, add butter and chopped shallots until softened. Whisk in flour, continually whisking for 3 minutes. Add warm milk, in a fast stream, whisking constantly to prevent lumps in the sauce and simmer. Continue to whisk until thick, about 3 to 4 minutes. Stir in chopped spinach, grated nutmeg, salt and black pepper to taste. Continue to stir until heated through.

Chef's Note:

You can save the blanching step if you chopped frozen spinach; there is no difference in taste.

The creamed spinach can be made a day ahead, cooled completely, and reheated over medium heat.

YORKSHIRE PUDDING

Yorkshire pudding is very similar to "Popovers." In any case, you may use the popover tins or molds for this dish. Be very careful when pouring the batter into the hot oil, and **DO NOT SPILL** the oil or batter into your very hot oven, or a fire may happen.

Yield: 6 puddings

Ingredients:
1 cup all-purpose flour
1 teaspoon salt
2 large eggs
1 cup whole milk
6 tablespoons reserved beef fat from Prime Rib
  or vegetable oil

Directions: In a blender or with a whisk, blend flour, salt, eggs and milk until just smooth; chill batter for 30 minutes.

Preheat oven to 425 degrees with a rack in the middle of oven and room above it. Place popover mold on a baking sheet for ease of movement. Spray or wipe insides and tops of molds with oil.

Place 1 tablespoon of the prime rib fat into each of the molds. Put baking sheet with molds into oven for 5 minutes to heat oil. Quickly pour ½ cup of batter into each mold and bake for about 18 minutes or until the Yorkshire Puddings are puffed and golden brown. Remove from mold with tongs and serve immediately.

Chef's Note:
I suggest purchasing Teflon or silicon popover molds, and even then, spray with oil and wipe excess before each use.

POTATOES GRATIN
Gratin Dauphinois

This classic potato dish is frequently served with prime rib. Depending on how rich or cheesy you like your potatoes, you could add a touch of sour cream or blue cheese in between the potato layers. Or make it a little lighter by using milk in place of the half & half or heavy cream (but why bother at this point).

Yield: 6 to 8 servings

Ingredients:

3 pounds Russet potatoes, medium size
2 tablespoons unsalted butter
1 medium garlic clove, crushed and pressed
1½ to 2 cups half & half
sea or kosher, to taste
freshly grated nutmeg, to taste
1 to 2 cups Gruyère or Parmesan cheese, grated
4 tablespoons crème fraîche or sour cream
¼ cup Parmesan cheese

Directions: Peel and wash the potatoes. Slice them into ⅛-inch rounds with a mandolin, food processor or sharp knife. Place potatoes in cold water until used.

Generously butter a heavy, shallow, gratin casserole baking dish or a 12-inch, cast-iron pan. Rub the dish with half of the crushed garlic. In a saucepan, add the half & half and the remaining garlic, some salt, black pepper and freshly grated nutmeg. Bring mixture to a simmer. Set aside.

Preheat oven to 350 degrees. Drain sliced potatoes and pat dry. Arrange an even overlapping layer on the bottom of the casserole. Season with salt and freshly ground black pepper. Sprinkle some Gruyère or Parmesan cheese on top of the potatoes. Arrange two more overlapping layers, using the same method; do not put any cheese on the top layer. Gently, press down the layers to compress and to remove any air. Pour in some of the half & half mixture and gently press again. Add the remaining half & half until it comes up just below the top layer of potatoes. Cover with foil. Place on a baking sheet and bake in oven for 1 hour or until the potatoes may be pierced easily with a small knife.

Raise the oven temperature to 425 degrees; remove foil; bake for 10 minutes or until the top layer of potatoes begins to brown. Remove from oven; add heavy cream to cover the top and place dabs of the crème fraîche or sour cream and sprinkle with Parmesan cheese. Return casserole to oven and bake for 15 to 20 minutes until the top is golden brown and bubbly. Remove from oven and let stand for 10 minutes. Cut into squares and serve.

Chef's Note:

You may also try using your favorite blue or Brie cheese, as well as habanero or pepper jack for a twist on a classical dish. Don't be afraid of steeping the half & half or heavy cream with more garlic or rosemary.

PRIME RIB
& AU JUS

There is no other cut of meat that says "party" like a whole prime rib. They are very costly and, depending on where you live, finding "prime" may be hard to do. Most places carry only "choice or select meat" but it's worth the hunt, if you can find "prime." It's even better if it's dry aged. If it's dry aged, it will be off-the-bone because the bones and fat cap are removed and discarded after the aging process. Also remember to remove both ends of the rib, as they will be quite tough from the aging, but the rest is culinary heaven, if it's cooked right, that is.

Yield: 8 servings

Ingredients:

1 9-pound beef prime rib roast, 4 ribs
2 tablespoons sea or kosher salt
2 tablespoons dried thyme
2 tablespoons freshly ground black pepper
2 tablespoons superfine sugar
2 tablespoons minced garlic

AU JUS

⅓ cup minced shallots
3½ cups canned beef broth
⅓ cup cognac
Roasting juices

Directions: Position rack in center of oven, and preheat to 450 degrees. Place beef's fat side up in a shallow roasting pan. Mix salt, thyme, pepper, superfine sugar and garlic together, mixing well. Sprinkle and rub spice mix all over roast; gently pat or rub it into the meat and fat.

Roast meat for 15 minutes. Reduce oven's heat to 350 degrees. Roast until meat thermometer, when inserted into the center of the roast, reads 125 degrees (this will give you a medium-rare) or 135 degrees for medium. Roast meat for about 2 hours and 45 minutes, checking temp at the two-hour mark. If meat is browning too quickly, tent loosely with foil.

When beef reaches desired temp of 125 or 135, remove from heat and place on carving platter to rest. Tent loosely with foil to keep warm while resting; the internal temperature of the meat will continue to rise during this period.

Pour off the pan's juices from roasting pan into a large glass measuring cup (DO NOT wash roasting pan). Place cup in freezer for 10 minutes. Spoon fat from measuring cup and reserve for Yorkshire Pudding and Au Jus. Reserve the juices.

Melt 1 tablespoon of the fat in roasting pan over medium-high heat; add shallots and sauté until translucent, scraping the brown bits in the pan. Remove from heat and add the canned beef broth and roasting juices. Add cognac and return to heat (it may ignite!). Let juices come to a boil and reduce to 2 cups of Au Jus. Transfer Au Jus to sauce boat and serve with meat.

Chef's Note: If roasting a "bone in" roast, carve the roast off the bones before cutting against the grain. Save those bones. Re-warm them with some barbecue sauce for lunch the next day. Trim off extra fat; render down for the fat in your Yorkshire puddings.